COLLINS

PHRASE BOOK & DICTIONARY

Greek

HarperCollins*Publishers*

Food section by Edite Vieira Phillips

Other languages in the *Collins Phrase Book & Dictionary* series:

FRENCH
GERMAN
GREEK
PORTUGUESE
RUSSIAN
SPANISH

These titles are also published in a language pack containing
60-minute cassette and phrase book

HarperCollins Publishers
P O Box, Glasgow G4 0NB
www.**fire**and**water**.com

First published 2000
Copyright © HarperCollins*Publishers*
Reprint 10 9 8 7 6 5 4 3 2 1
Printed in Italy by Amadeus SpA

ISBN 0 00-472072 5

INTRODUCTION

Your *Collins Phrase Book & Dictionary* is a handy, quick-reference guide that will help you make the most of your stay abroad. Its clear layout will save you valuable time when you need that crucial word or phrase.

There are three main sections in this book:

Practical topics arranged thematically with an opening section **KEY TALK** containing vital phrases that should stand you in good stead in most situations.

> ## PHRASES
> **Short easy phrases that can be adapted for your situation**
>
> *practical tips are highlighted in yellow boxes*
>
> SIGNS ARE IN GREEN BOXES
>
> replies you might hear are highlighted in red boxes

> ## FOOD SECTION
> **Phrases for ordering drinks and food**
> **A description of Greek and Cypriot food and drinks**
> **Menu reader**

DICTIONARY

English-Greek	Greek-English	signs highlighted

And finally, a short **GRAMMAR** section explaining how the language works.

So, just flick through the pages to find the information you need. Why not start with a look at pronouncing Greek on page 6. From there on the going is easy with your *Collins Phrase Book & Dictionary*.

CONTENTS

PRONOUNCING GREEK

*In the pronunciation system in this book, Greek sounds are repre-
sented by spellings of the nearest possible sounds in English.
When you read the pronunciation, sound the letters as if you were
reading English (but make sure you also pronounce vowels at the
end of a word). The vowels in **heavy type** show where the stress
falls (in the Greek script it is marked with an accent).The following
notes should help:*

	REMARKS	EXAMPLE	PRONOUNCED
gh	like **r** at back of throat	γάλα	<u>gh</u>ala
dh	like **th** in this	δάχτυλο	<u>dh</u>akhteelo
th	like **th** in thin	θέατρο	<u>th</u>eatro
ks	like **x** in fox	ξένος	<u>ks</u>enos
r	slightly trilled **r**	ρόδα	<u>r</u>odha
kh	like **ch** in loch	χάνω	<u>kh</u>ano
	like a rough **h** before e or ee	χέρι	<u>kh</u>eree

Here are a few tricky letter combinations:

αι	m<u>e</u>t	**e**	γυναίκα	gheen<u>e</u>ka
αυ	c<u>af</u>é	**af**	αυτό	<u>af</u>to
	or h<u>av</u>e	**av**	αύριο	<u>a</u>vreeo
ει	m<u>ee</u>t	**ee**	είκοσι	<u>ee</u>kosee
ευ	<u>ef</u>fect	**ef**	Δευτέρα	dh<u>ef</u>tera
	or <u>ev</u>ery	**ev**	Ευρώπη	<u>e</u>vropee
γγ	ha<u>ng</u>	**ng**	Αγγλία	ang<u>lee</u>a
γκ	<u>g</u>et	**g**	γκάζι	<u>g</u>azee
	ha<u>ng</u>	**ng**	άγκυρα	<u>a</u>ngeera
ντ	ha<u>nd</u>	**nd**	αντίο	and<u>ee</u>o
	<u>d</u>og	**d**	ντομάτα	dom<u>a</u>ta
μπ	<u>b</u>ag	**b**	μπλούζα	<u>b</u>looza
οι	m<u>ee</u>t	**ee**	πλοίο	pl<u>ee</u>o
ου	m<u>oo</u>n	**oo**	ούζο	<u>oo</u>zo

*The letters η, ι, υ, οι, and ει have the same sound **ee** and αι and ε
have the same sound **e** (as in m**e**t). You should also note that the
Greek question mark is a semi-colon, i.e. ;.*

*Greek has two forms of address, formal and informal. The informal is used among family and friends. You will hear γειά σου (ya soo), meaning **hi** and **bye**, among friends and young people.*

yes	**no**	**that's fine**
ne	okhee	endaksee
ναι	όχι	εντάξει

please	**thank you**	
parakalo	efkhareesto	parakalo
παρακαλώ	ευχαριστώ	**παρακαλώ**
		don't mention it

hello / goodbye	**hello**	**good night**
ya sas / ya sas	kherete	kalee neekhta
γειά σας / γειά σας	χαίρετε	καλή νύχτα

good morning	**good evening**
kaleemera	kaleespera
καλημέρα	καλησπέρα

excuse me / sorry	**that's very kind**
seeghnomee	polee efyeneeko ek meroo sas
συγνώμη	πολύ ευγενικό εκ μέρου σας

Here's an easy way to ask for things... just add parakalo (please)

a...	**a coffee**	**2 coffees**
enan... (*'o' words*)	enan kafe	dheeo kafedhes
έναν...	έναν καφέ	δύο καφέδες
meea... (*'η' words*)	**a beer**	**2 beers**
μία...	meea beera	dheeo beeres
	μία μπίρα	δύο μπίρες
ena... (*'το' words*)	**a bottle**	**2 bottles**
ένα...	ena bookalee	dheeo bookaleea
	ένα μπουκάλι	δύο μπουκάλια

a coffee and two beers, please
enan kafe ke dheeo beeres parakalo
έναν καφέ και δύο μπίρες, παρακαλώ

KEY TALK

I'd like...
tha eethela...
θα ήθελα...

we'd like...
tha thelame...
θα θέλαμε...

I'd like an ice cream
tha eethela ena paghoto
θα ήθελα ένα παγωτό

we'd like to go to Athens
tha thelame na pame steen atheena
θα θέλαμε να πάμε στην Αθήνα

do you have...?
ekhete...?
έχετε...;

do you have any milk?
ekhete ghala
έχετε γάλα;

do you have stamps?
ekhete ghramatoseema
έχετε γραμματόσημα;

do you have a map?
ekhete ena khartee?
έχετε ένα χάρτη;

do you have fruit?
ekhete froota?
έχετε φρούτα;

how much is it?
poso kanee
πόσο κάνει;

how much does ... cost?
poso kosteezee o / ee / to...?
πόσο κοστίζει ο / η / το...;

how much is the wine?
poso kanee to krasee
πόσο κάνει το κρασί;

how much does the ticket cost?
poso kosteezee to eeseeteereeo
πόσο κοστίζει το εισιτήριο;

how much is a kilo?
poso kanee to keelo
πόσο κάνει το κιλό;

how much is one?
poso kanee to ena
πόσο κάνει το ένα;

ΝΤΟΜΑΤΕΣ....................το κιλό	TOMATOES PER KILO
ΑΧΛΑΔΙΑ........................το κιλό	PEARS PER KILO
ΠΟΡΤΟΚΑΛΙΑ................το κιλό	ORANGES PER KILO

where is / are...?
poo **ee**ne...
πού είναι...;

where is the toilet?
poo **ee**ne ee tooa**le**ta
πού είναι η τουαλέτα;

where are the children?
poo **ee**ne ta ped**ya**
πού είναι τα παιδιά;

ΓΥΝΑΙΚΩΝ	LADIES
ΑΝΔΡΕΣ	GENTS

ΕΙΣΟΔΟΣ	ENTRANCE
ΕΞΟΔΟΣ	EXIT

is there...?
ee**par**khee...
υπάρχει...;

are there...?
ee**par**khoon...
υπάρχουν...;

is there a taverna?
ee**par**khee **me**ea ta**ver**na
υπάρχει μία ταβέρνα;

where is there a chemist?
poo **ee**ne **e**na farma**kee**o
πού είναι ένα φαρμακείο;

are there any rooms?
ee**par**khoon dhoma**tee**a
υπάρχουν δωμάτια;

is there a swimming pool?
ee**par**khee pee**see**na
υπάρχει πισίνα;

there is no...
dhen **e**khee...
δεν έχει...

there is no hot water
dhen **e**khee zes**to** ne**ro**
δεν έχει ζεστό νερό

there is no bread
dhen **e**khee pso**mee**
δεν έχει ψωμί

I need...
khree**a**zome...
χρειάζομαι...

I need a doctor
khree**a**zome **e**nan yat**ro**
χρειάζομαι έναν γιατρό

I need a taxi
khree**a**zome tak**see**
χρειάζομαι ταξί

KEY TALK

can I...?
boro na...
μπορώ να...;

can we...?
boroome na ...
μπορούμε να...;

can I pay?
boro na pleeroso
μπορώ να πληρώσω;

can we eat?
boroome na fame
μπορούμε να φάμε;

where can I...?
poo boro na...
πού μπορώ να...;

where can I buy bread?
poo boro na aghoraso psomee
πού μπορώ να αγοράσω ψωμί;

where can I get tickets?
poo boro na aghoraso eeseeteereea
πού μπορώ να αγοράσω εισιτήρια;

boreete na aghorasete eeseeteereea sto pereeptero
μπορείτε να αγοράσετε εισιτήρια στο περίπτερο
you can buy tickets at the kiosk

when?
pote
πότε;

at what time...?
tee ora...
τι ώρα...;

when does it leave?
pote fevyee
πότε φεύγει;

when does it arrive?
pote ftanee
πότε φτάνει;

when does it open?
pote aneeyee
πότε ανοίγει;

when does it close?
pote kleenee
πότε κλείνει;

yesterday
khtes
χτες

today
seemera
σήμερα

tomorrow
avreeo
αύριο

this morning
seemera to proee
σήμερα το πρωί

this afternoon
seemera to apoyefma
σήμερα το απόγευμα

tonight
apopse
απόψε

10

ΘΕΡΙΝΟ ΩΡΑΡΙΟ	SUMMER TIMETABLE
ΧΕΙΜΕΡΙΝΟ ΩΡΑΡΙΟ	WINTER TIMETABLE
ΚΛΕΙΣΤΟ ΛΟΓΩ ΔΙΑΚΟΠΩΝ	CLOSED FOR HOLIDAYS
ΚΛΕΙΣΤΟ ΛΟΓΩ ΑΡΓΙΑΣ	CLOSED FOR RESTDAY

ΔΕΥΤ	MON
ΤΡ	TUE
ΤΕΤ	WED
ΠΕ	THU
ΠΑΡ	FRI
ΣΑΒ	SAT
ΚΥΡ	SUN

is it open?
eene aneekto
είναι ανοικτό;

is it closed?
eene kleesto
είναι κλειστό;

ΑΝΟΙΚΤΟ	OPEN
ΚΛΕΙΣΤΟ	CLOSED
ΔΕΥΤ – ΣΑΒ	WEEKDAY (Mon-Sat)
Κυριακές και γιορτές	HOLIDAY/ SUNDAY

aneekto stees enea pm
ανοικτό στις 9 πμ
it opens at 9 am

to mooseeo eene kleesto teen dheftera
το μουσείο είναι κλειστό την Δευτέρα
the museum is closed on Mondays

GETTING TO KNOW PEOPLE

If you don't know a person's surname you can simply address them as κύριε *(keereeye for a man) and* κυρία *(keereea for a woman).*

how are you?
tee kanete
τι κάνετε;

fine, thanks, and you?
kala, efkhareesto, esees
καλά, ευχαριστώ, εσείς;

my name is...
me lene...
με λένε...

what is your name?
pos sas lene
πώς σας λένε;

I don't understand
dhen katalaveno
δεν καταλαβαίνω

do you speak English?
meelate angleeka
μιλάτε αγγλικά;

11

MONEY – changing

ΣΥΝΑΛΛΑΓΜΑ	BUREAU DE CHANGE
ATM	CASH DISPENSER
δρχ or Δρχ	DRACHMAS

Banks are generally open from 8am–2pm Mon–Fri, and cash dispensers are becoming more widespread. Cash is the preferred method of payment and you can sometimes negotiate a reduction if you pay in cash. There is an automatic conversion point in Syntagma Square.

where can I change money?
poo boro na alakso khreemata
πού μπορώ να αλλάξω χρήματα;

where is there a bank?
poo eene meea trapeza
πού είναι μία τράπεζα;

where is there a bureau de change?
poo eene ena enalakteereeo seenalaghmatos
πού είναι ένα εναλλακτήριο συναλλάγματος;

when does the bank open?
pote aneeyee ee trapeza
πότε ανοίγει η τράπεζα;

when does the bank close?
pote kleenee ee trapeza
πότε κλείνει η τράπεζα;

where is there a cash dispenser?
poo ekhee ena ey tee em
πού έχει ένα ΑΤΜ;

I want to cash these traveller's cheques
tha eethela na alakso afta ta takseedhyoteeka tsek
θα ήθελα να αλλάξω αυτά τα ταξιδιωτικά τσεκ

what is the rate for...?
pya eene ee eesoteemeea ya...
ποια είναι η ισοτιμία για...;

pounds
tee leera vretaneeas
τη λίρα Βρετανίας

dollars
to dholareeo
το δολάριο

I want to change £50
tha eethela na alakso peneenda leeres vretaneeas
θα ήθελα να αλλάξω 50 λίρες Βρετανίας

TAMEIO CASH DESK   **ΦΠΑ** VAT

If you are visiting more remote areas, away from tourist spots, you should carry enough cash to get by, particularly at the weekend, in case banks and bureaux de change close early on a Friday.

how much is it?
poso kanee
πόσο κάνει;

where do I pay?
poo pleerono
πού πληρώνω;

I want to pay
thelo na pleeroso
θέλω να πληρώσω

how much do I have to pay?
poso prepee na pleeroso
πόσο πρέπει να πληρώσω;

can I pay by credit card?
boro na pleeroso me peestoteekee karta
μπορώ να πληρώσω με πιστωτική κάρτα;

do you accept traveller's cheques?
dhekheste takseedhyoteeka tsek
δέχεστε ταξιδιωτικά τσεκ;

how much is it...?	**per person**	**per night**	**per kilo**
poso kanee...	*kat atomo*	*too vradyoo*	*to keelo*
πόσο κάνει...;	κατ᾽ άτομο	του βραδυού	το κιλό

I need a receipt
khreeazome teen apodheeksee
χρειάζομαι την απόδειξη

do I need to pay a deposit?
khreeazete na dhoso prokatavolee
χρειάζεται να δώσω προκαταβολή;

pleeroste sto tameeo
πληρώστε στο ταμείο
pay at the cash desk

AIRPORT

ΑΦΗΞΕΙΣ	ARRIVALS
ΑΝΑΧΩΡΗΣΕΙΣ	DEPARTURES
ΑΠΟΣΚΕΥΕΣ	BAGGAGE RECLAIM
ΠΤΗΣΗ	FLIGHT
ΚΑΘΥΣΤΕΡΗΣΗ	DELAY

to the airport, please
sto aerodhromeeo parakalo
στο αεροδρόμιο, παρακαλώ

how do I get into town?
pos boro na pao sto kentro tees polees
πώς μπορώ να πάω στο κέντρο της πόλης;

where do I get the bus to the town centre?
apo poo perno to leoforeeo ya to kentro tees polees
από πού παίρνω το λεωφορείο για το κέντρο της πόλης;

how much is it...?	**to the centre**	**to the airport**
poso kanee...	*ya to kentro*	*ya to aerodhromeeo*
πόσο κάνει...;	για το κέντρο	για το αεροδρόμιο

where do I check in for...?
poo eene o elengkhos eeseeteereeon ya...
πού είναι ο έλεγχος εισιτηρίων για...;

which gate is it for the flight to...?
pya eene ee eksodhos tees pteesees ya...
ποια είναι η έξοδος της πτήσης για...;

---

epeeveevasee steen eesodho...(number)
επιβίβαση στην είσοδο...
boarding will take place at gate number...

teleftea kleesee
τελευταία κλήση
last call

ee pteesee eene katheestereemenee
η πτήση είναι καθυστερημένη
the flight is delayed

CUSTOMS & PASSPORTS

ΤΕΛΩΝΕΙΟ	CUSTOMS
EU ΔΙΑΒΑΤΗΡΙΑ	EU CITIZENS

With the single European market, passengers arriving from a member state of the European Union are subject only to highly selective spot checks and they can go through the blue customs channel. Remember that Cyprus is not a member of the EU and therefore customs restrictions apply.

I have nothing to declare
dhen ekho teepote ya dheelosee
δεν έχω τίποτε για δήλωση

here is...   **my passport**   **my visa**
afto eene...   to dheeavateerceo moo   ee veeza moo
αυτό είναι...   το διαβατήριό μου   η βίζα μου

do I have to pay duty on this?
prepee na pleeroso foro yee afto
πρέπει να πληρώσω φόρο γι' αυτό;

it's for my own personal use
eene ya prosopeekee khreesee
είναι για προσωπική χρήση

the children are on this passport
ta pedya eene se afto to dheeavateereeo
τα παιδιά είναι σε αυτό το διαβατήριο

this is the baby's passport
afto eene to dheeavateereeo too moroo
αυτό είναι το διαβατήριο του μωρού

I'm...   **British** (m/f)   **Australian** (m/f)
eeme...   vretanos / vretaneedha   afstralos / afstraleedha
είμαι...   Βρετανός / Βρετανίδα   Αυστραλός / Αυστραλίδα

ASKING THE WAY – questions

excuse me
seeghnomee
συγνώμη

where is the nearest...?
poo eene to kondeenotero...
πού είναι το κοντινότερο...;

how do I get to...?
pos boro na pao sto (with ο and το words) / **stee** (with η words)...
πώς μπορώ να πάω στο / στη...;

is this the right way to...?
eeme sto sosto dhromo ya...
είμαι στο σωστό δρόμο για...;

the...
o (masc.) / *ee* (fem.) / *to* (neuter)...
ο / η / το...

can I walk there?
eene konda me ta podheea
είναι κοντά με τα πόδια;

is there a bus that goes there?
eeparkhee kapyo leoforeeo poo peeyenee ekee
υπάρχει κάποιο λεωφορείο που πηγαίνει εκεί;

we're looking for...
psakhnoome ya to (with ο and το words) / **tee** (with η words)...
ψάχνουμε για το / τη ...

we're lost
khatheekame
χαθήκαμε

can you show me on the map?
boreete na moo to dheeksete sto khartee
μπορείτε να μου το δείξετε στο χάρτη;

where is...?
poo eene...
πού είναι...;

is it far?
eene makreea
είναι μακριά;

answers – ASKING THE WAY

It's no use being able to ask the way if you're not going to understand the directions you get. We've tried to anticipate the likely answers, so listen carefully for these key phrases.

eftheea brosta
ευθεία μπροστά
keep going straight ahead

prepee na yeereesete peeso
πρέπει να γυρίσετε πίσω
you have to turn round

streepste...
στρίψτε...
turn...

dheksya
δεξιά
right

areestera
αριστερά
left

peeyenete...
πηγαίνετε...
go...

pros...
προς...
towards...

seenekheeste...
συνεχίστε...
keep going...

eos...
εως...
as far as...

parte...
πάρτε...
take...

ton proto dhromo dheksya
τον πρώτο δρόμο δεξιά
the first road on the right

ton dheftero dhromo areestera
τον δεύτερο δρόμο αριστερά
the second road on the left

dheeaskheeste...
διασχίστε...
cross...

teen plateea
την πλατεία
the square

eene meta ta fanareea
είναι μετά τα φανάρια
it's after the traffic lights

BUS/TROLLEY-BUS

Buy your bus tickets in advance at newspaper kiosks, tobacconists showing the bus company logo or at the ticket booths of the transport company. On boarding the bus you must immediately stamp your ticket in the orange machine which is usually by the front or rear doors. In Athens the same tickets are used for both bus and trolley-bus. Special tickets need to be bought on the airport bus and for the underground.

where is the bus station?
poo eene o stathmos leoforeeon
πού είναι ο σταθμός λεωφορείων;

I want to go...	**to the station**	**to the museum**
thelo na pao...	*sto stathmo*	*sto mooseeo*
θέλω να πάω...	στο σταθμό	στο μουσείο
	to the Acropolis	**to the Plaka**
	steen akropolee	*steen plaka*
	στην Ακρόπολη	στην Πλάκα

does this bus go to...?
afto to leoforeeo peeyenee sto / stee...
αυτό το λεωφορείο πηγαίνει στο / στη...;

which bus do I take?
pyo leoforeeo tha paro
ποιο λεωφορείο θα πάρω;

where does the bus go from?
apo poo perna to leoforeeo
από πού περνά το λεωφορείο;

how often are the buses?
kathe pote ekhee leoforeeo
κάθε πότε έχει λεωφορείο;

can you please tell me when to get off?
boreete na moo peete pote na katevo
μπορείτε να μου πείτε πότε να κατεβώ;

BUS/COACH

For long-distance bus travel buy your ticket in the local bus agency.
In small places this is often in the **καφενείον** (kafeneeon), the coffee
shop. The Greek bus service for long-distance routes is called **ΚΤΕΛ**
(KTEL). Note that smoking is prohibited on their services.

where is the KTEL office?
*poo **ee**ne to praktor**ee**o too ktel*
πού είναι το πρακτορείο του ΚΤΕΛ;

1 ticket	**2 tickets**
ena eeseet**ee**reeo	dh**ee**o eeseet**ee**reea
ένα εισιτήριο	δύο εισιτήρια

a return ticket
e**na eeseet**ee**reeo me epeestrof**ee
ένα εισιτήριο με επιστροφή

to Thessaloniki	**to Patra**
*stee thesalon**ee**kee*	*steen **p**atra*
στη Θεσσαλονίκη	στην Πάτρα

how much does it cost to...?
*p**o**so kost**ee**zee ya...*
πόσο κοστίζει για...;

are there any discounts for students / pensioners?
***e**khee eedh**ee**ka eeseet**ee**reea ya feet**ee**tes / seendaksy**oo**khoos*
έχει ειδικά εισιτήρια για φοιτητές / συνταξιούχους;

where does the coach leave?
*ap**o** poo pern**a** to lefor**ee**o*
από πού περνά το λεωφορείο;

when does the coach leave
*p**o**te f**e**vyee to lefor**ee**o*
πότε φεύγει το λεωφορείο;

how long does it take to...?
*pyee **o**ra k**a**nee ya...*
ποιη ώρα κάνει για...;

TRAIN

ΕΙΣΙΤΗΡΙΑ	TICKETS
ΠΛΗΡΟΦΟΡΙΕΣ	INFORMATION
ΑΝΑΧΩΡΗΣΕΙΣ	DEPARTURES
ΑΦΙΞΕΙΣ	ARRIVALS
ΠΛΑΤΦΟΡΜΑ	PLATFORM

There is only a fairly small network of trains on mainland Greece.
Faster Intercity trains connect Athens with Thessaloniki and
Patras. Slower local trains run in the Peloponnese and Thessaly
and Macedonia.

where is the station?
*poo **ee**ne o stathm**o**s tr**e**noo*
πού είναι ο σταθμός τρένου;

to the station, please
*sto stathm**o** parakal**o***
στο σταθμό παρακαλώ

a single to...
*ena apl**o** eeseet**ee**reeo ya...*
ένα απλό εισιτήριο για...

2 singles to...
*dh**ee**o apl**a** eeseet**ee**reea ya...*
δύο απλά εισιτήρια για...

a return to...
*ena eeseet**ee**reeo me epeestrof**ee** ya...*
ένα εισιτήριο με επιστροφή για...

2 returns to...
*dh**ee**o eeseet**ee**reea me epeestrof**ee** ya...*
δύο εισιτήρια με επιστροφή για...

lst / 2nd class
*pr**o**tee / dh**e**fteree th**e**see*
πρώτη / δεύτερη θέση

smoking
*kapneest**o**n*
καπνιστών

non smoking
*mee kapneest**o**n*
μη καπνιστών

is this the train for...?
*eene aft**o** to tr**e**no ya...*
είναι αυτό το τρένο για...;

is this seat free?
*eene ee th**e**see el**e**vtheree*
είναι η θέση ελεύθερη;

METRO

ΜΕΤΡΟ	UNDERGROUND
ΕΙΣΟΔΟΣ	ENTRANCE
ΕΞΟΔΟΣ	EXIT
ΚΑΡΤΑ ΑΠΕΡΙΟΡΙΣΤΩΝ ΔΙΑΔΡΟΜΩΝ	SEASON TICKET HOLDERS

The 'old' Athens underground is called **Ηλεκτρικό** *(eelektreeko)
and runs to the port of Piraeus. Tickets for the new metro* **Αττικό
μετρό** *(ateeko metro) are different from bus tickets and can be
bought at ticket booths and machines in the underground. One
day tickets cost 1,000 drachmas.*

where is the metro station?   *(for old electric line)*
*poo **ee**ne o sta**thm**os too me**tro***   **too eelektreek**oo**
πού είναι ο σταθμός του μετρό;   του ηλεκτρικού;

a ticket / 4 tickets, please
*ena eeseet**ee**reeo / tessera eeseet**ee**reea parakal**o***
ένα εισιτήριο / τέσσερα εισιτήρια παρακαλώ

do you have an underground map?
*ekhete **e**nan khartee me tees ghramm**e**s too me**tro***
έχετε έναν χάρτη με τις γραμμές του μετρό;

I want to go to...   **can I go by underground?**
thelo na pao sto / stee...   *boro na pao me to metro*
θέλω να πάω στο / στη...   μπορώ να πάω με το μετρό;

do I have to change?   **where?**
prepee na alakso treno   *poo*
πρέπει να αλλάξω τρένο;   πού;

which line do I take?
*pya ghramm**ee** prepee na paro*
ποια γραμμή πρέπει να πάρω;

which is the station for Syntagma?
*pyos **ee**ne o sta**thm**os ya to s**ee**ndagma*
ποιος είναι ο σταθμός για το Σύνταγμα;

TAXI

Usually taxis should be hailed in the street. Radio taxis and taxis from and to the airports, bus and train stations charge an extra fee. Taxis are yellow in Athens, blue and white in Thessaloniki and usually grey in smaller towns. Make sure the meter is on tariff 1. Tariff 2 is for after midnight and is double the price. Tipping is not necessary, but appreciated.

to the airport, please
sto aerodhromeeo parakalo
στο αεροδρόμιο, παρακαλώ

please take me to this address
se afteen teen dheeevtheensee parakalo
σε αυτήν την διεύθυνση, παρακαλώ

how much will it cost?
poso kosteezee
πόσο κοστίζει;

it's too much
eene polee akreeva
είναι πολύ ακριβά

how much is to the centre?
poso kosteezee ya to kentro
πόσο κοστίζει για το κέντρο;

where can I get a taxi?
poo boro na vro taksee
πού μπορώ να βρω ταξί;

please order me a taxi
parakalo kaleste ena taksee
παρακαλώ καλέστε ένα ταξί

can I have a receipt?
boreete na moo dhosete apodheeksee
μπορείτε να μου δώσετε απόδειξη;

I've nothing smaller
dheesteekhos dhen ekho pseela
δυστυχώς δεν έχω ψηλά

keep the change
krateeste ta resta
κρατήστε τα ρέστα

The ferry service to the Greek islands is extensive. There are four classes of ticket: first, second, third and tourist. Foot passengers do not have to book tickets in advance, but if you plan to take a push bike or motorbike you must book in advance. Hydrofoils are faster but tickets are more expensive. Some hydrofoils now take cars and motorbikes.

1 ticket	**2 tickets**	**single**	**round trip**
ena eeseeteereeo	*dheeo eseeteereea*	*apla*	*me epeestrofee*
ένα εισιτήριο	δύο εισιτήρια	απλά	με επιστροφή

is there a tourist ticket?
eeparkhee eedheeko tooreesteeko eeseeteereeo
υπάρχει ειδικό τουριστικό εισιτήριο;

is there a ticket for students / pensioners?
ekhee eedheeka eeseeteereea ya feeteetes / seendaksyookhoos
έχει ειδικά εισιτήρια για φοιτητές / συνταξιούχους;

when does the ferry leave?
pote fevyee to pleeo
πότε φεύγει το πλοίο;

do you have a timetable?
ekhete ta dhromologhya
έχετε τα δρομολόγια;

is there a restaurant on board?
ekhee esteeatoreeo mesa
έχει εστιατόριο μέσα;

can we hire a boat?
boroome na neekyasoome meea varka
μπορούμε να νοικιάσουμε μία βάρκα;

are there any boat trips?
proteenete kapyes dheeadhromes me teen varka
προτείνετε κάποιες διαδρομές με την βάρκα;

CAR – driving/parking

ΟΛΕΣ ΤΙΣ ΚΑΤΕΥΘΥΝΣΕΙΣ	ALL ROUTES
ΕΞΟΔΟΣ	EXIT
ΑΥΤΟΚΙΝΗΤΟΔΡΟΜΟΣ	MOTORWAY
ΔΙΟΔΙΑ	TOLL
ΑΠΑΓΟΡΕΥΕΤΑΙ ΤΟ ΠΑΡΚΑΡΙΣΜΑ	NO PARKING
ΚΕΝΤΡΟ	CITY CENTRE

To drive in Greece visitors must be at least 18 years old and have a valid pink EU licence. An international driving licence is required for other nationals. Tolls are payable on most sections of the motorway (αυτοκινητόδρομος aftokeeneetodhromos) at toll booths. Fees range from 500 to 1,000 drachmas. Keep your receipt in case the motorway police stops you. In cities you can park in the street or in private parking areas which charge by the day or hour. In Cyprus you drive on the left.

can I park here?
boro na parkaro edho
μπορώ να παρκάρω εδώ;

where is the ticket machine?
poo eene to parkometro
πού είναι το παρκόμετρο;

where can I park?
poo boro na parkaro
πού μπορώ να παρκάρω;

is there a car park near here?
eeparkhee kapyo parking edho konda
υπάρχει κάποιο πάρκινγκ εδώ κοντά;

how long can I park here?
ya posee ora boro na parkaro edho
για πόση ώρα μπορώ να παρκάρω εδώ;

we're going to....
peeyenoome sto / stee...
πηγαίνουμε στο / στη...

what's the best route?
pos tha pame kaleetera
πώς θα πάμε καλύτερα;

is the pass open?
eene o dhromos aneektos
είναι ο δρόμος ανοικτός;

is the road good?
eene o dhromos kalos
είναι ο δρόμος καλός;

ΣΟΥΠΕΡ / SUPER	4 STAR
ΑΜΟΛΥΒΔΗ	UNLEADED
ΝΤΙΣΕΛ / DIESEL	DIESEL
ΒΕΝΖΙΝΗ	PETROL

Motorway petrol stations are usually open 24 hours a day, but off the motorway opening hours are restricted and petrol stations close at night time and on Sundays and public holidays. There is no self-service.

is there a petrol station near here?
eeparkhee venzeenadheeko edho konda
υπάρχει βενζινάδικο εδώ κοντά;

fill it up, please
yemeeste to parakalo
γεμίστε το, παρακαλώ

unleaded
amoleevdhee
αμόλυβδη

five thousand drachmas of unleaded
pende kheelyadhes amoleevdhee
πέντε χιλιάδες αμόλυβδη

where is the air line?
poo ekhee aera
πού έχει αέρα;

can you wash the windscreen?
boreete na pleenete to parbreez
μπορείτε να πλήνετε το παρμπρίζ;

please check...
boreete na eleghkhete...
μπορείτε να ελέγχετε...

the tyre pressure
teen peeyesee sta lasteekha
την πίεση στα λαστιχά

the oil
ta ladheea
τα λάδια

the water
to nero
το νερό

ola endaksee
όλα εντάξει
everything is ok

CAR – problems/breakdown

If you break down on the motorway you can use one of the emergency phones for assistance or get hold of one of the auto-mobile assistance services ΕΛΠΑ (ELPA) or Express Service.

I've broken down
khalase to aftokeeneeto moo
χάλασε το αυτοκίνητό μου

I'm on my own *(female)*
eeme monee moo
είμαι μόνη μου

there are children in the car
ekho pedya sto aftokeeneeto
έχω παιδιά στο αυτοκίνητο

where is the nearest garage? *(for repairs)*
poo eene to pyo kondeeno garaz
πού είναι το πιο κοντινό γκαράζ;

is it serious?
eene sovaro
είναι σοβαρό;

I don't have a spare tyre
dhen ekho rezerva
δεν έχω ρεζέρβα

have you the parts?
ekhete ta andalakteeka
έχετε τα ανταλλακτικά;

could you please help me to change the tyre
boreete na me voeetheesete na alakso lasteekho
μπορείτε να με βοηθήσετε να αλλάξω λάστιχο;

when will it be ready?
pote tha eene eteemo
πότε θα είναι έτοιμο;

how much will it cost?
poso tha kosteesee
πόσο θα κοστίσει;

the car won't start
ee meekhanee dhen ksekeena
η μηχανή δεν ξεκινά

the battery is flat
ee batareea eene adheea
η μπαταρία είναι άδεια

the engine is overheating
afksanete ee thermokraseea tees mekhanees
αυξάνεται η θερμοκρασία της μηχανής

I have a flat tyre
me epyase lasteekho
με έπιασε λαστιχο

can you replace the windscreen?
boreete na ftyaksete to parbreez
μπορείτε να φτιάξετε το παρμπρίζ;

RENT A CAR / ΕΝΟΙΚΙΑΣΕΙΣ ΑΥΤΟΚΙΝΗΤΩΝ   CAR HIRE

To hire a car in Greece you must be over 21 and have held a full driver's licence for at least a year. Car hire is quite expensive and it may be cheaper to make your arrangements before you go.

I want to hire a car	**for one day**	**for ... days**
thelo na neekyaso ena aftokeeneeto	*ya meea mera*	*ya ... meres*
θέλω να νοικιάσω ένα αυτοκίνητο	για μία μέρα	για ... μέρες

what is included in the insurance?
tee pereelamvanete steen asfaleea
τι περιλαμβάνεται στην ασφάλεια;

we want to take out additional insurance
thelo na paro prosthetee asfaleea
θέλω να πάρω πρόσθετη ασφάλεια

I want a...	**large**	**small**	**car**
proteemo ena...	*meghalo*	*meekro*	*aftokeeneeto*
προτιμώ ένα ...	μεγάλο	μικρό	αυτοκίνητο

what do we do if we break down?
tee prepee na kanoome se pereeptosee provleematos
τι πρέπει να κάνουμε σε περίπτωση προβλήματος;

where do I have to return the car to?	**by what time?**
poo prepee na epeestrepso to aftokeeneeto	*tee ora*
πού πρέπει να επιστρέψω το αυτοκίνητο;	τι ώρα;

I'd like to leave it in...
proteemo na to afeeso sto / stee...
προτιμώ να το αφήσω στο / στη...

where are the documents?
poo eene ee adheea keekloforeeas ke ee asfaleea
πού είναι η άδεια κυκλοφορίας και η ασφαλεία;

SHOPPING – holiday

Shops are usually open 8.30am–3.30pm and 5–8 pm Mon–Fri, and 8.30–3.30pm on Saturday. It is worth asking at kiosks for what you want as they are open till late and often sell a huge range of goods, not just newspapers and magazines. In Cyprus shops are closed on Wednesdays and Saturday afternoons.

do you sell...?
ekhete...
έχετε...;

stamps
ghrammatoseema
γραμματόσημα

batteries for this
batareees yee afto
μπαταρίες γι' αυτό

where can I find...?
poo na vro...
πού να βρω...;

a colour film
ena film eghkhromo
ένα φιλμ έγχρωμο

10 stamps
dheka ghramatoseema
δέκα γραμμάτοσημα

for postcards
ya kartes
για κάρτες

to Britain
ya angleea
για Αγγλία

a tape for this camcorder, please
meea kaseta ya afteen teen kamera parakalo
μία κασέτα για αυτήν την κάμερα, παρακαλώ

I'm looking for a present
psakhno ya ena dhoro
ψάχνω για ένα δώρο

have you something cheaper?
ekhete katee pyo ftheeno
έχετε κάτι πιο φθηνό;

it's a gift
eene ya dhoro
είναι για δώρο

please wrap it up
dheeploste to ya dhoro parakalo
διπλώστε το για δώρο, παρακαλώ

is there a market?
ekhee laeekee aghora
έχει λαϊκή αγορά;

which day?
pya mera
ποια μέρα;

clothes – SHOPPING

WOMEN		MEN		SHOES			
UK	EU	UK	EU	UK	EU	UK	EU
8	36	36	46	2	35	7	41
10	38	38	48	3	36	8	42
12	40	40	50	4	37	9	43
14	42	42	52	5	38	10	44
16	44	44	54	6	39	11	45
18	46	46	56	7	41	12	46

can I try this on?
boro na to dhokeemaso
μπορώ να το δοκιμάσω;

it's too big for me
moo eene meghalo
μου είναι μεγάλο

it's too small for me
moo eene polee steno
μου είναι πολύ στενό

it's too expensive
eene polee akreevo
είναι πολύ ακριβό

I'll take this one
tha to paro
θα το πάρω

I take a size ... shoe
foro ... noomero
φορώ ... νούμερο

I like it
moo aresee
μου αρέσει

I don't like it
dhen moo aresee
δεν μου αρέσει

have you a smaller one?
ekhete meekrotero noomero
έχετε μικρότερο νούμερο;

have you a larger one?
ekhete meghaleetero noomero
έχετε μεγαλύτερο νούμερο;

do you have this in my size?
ekhete afto sto noomero moo
έχετε αυτό στο νούμερό μου;

can you give me a discount?
tha moo kanete kaleeteree teemee
θα μου κάνετε καλύτερη τιμή;

tee noomero forate
τι νούμερο φοράτε;
what size are you?

tee noomero papootsyoo forate
τι νούμερο παπουτσιού φοράτε;
what shoe size do you take?

SHOPPING – food

ΦΟΥΡΝΟΣ BAKER'S	**SUPERMARKET** SUPERMARKET
ΚΡΕΟΠΩΛΕΙΟ BUTCHER'S	ΠΑΝΤΟΠΩΛΕΙΟ GROCER'S

*Most towns will have a market at least one day a week where
you can buy fresh fruit, vegetables and other local produce. They
are usually open from early morning till about 1.30pm. The price
of food starts to fall the nearer it gets to closing time.*

where can I buy...?
poo bo**ro** na aghora**so**...
πού μπορώ να αγοράσω...;

fruit
fr**oo**ta
φρούτα

bread
pso**mee**
ψωμί

milk
gha**la**
γάλα

where is the supermarket?
poo **ee**ne to super**mar**ket
πού είναι το σουπερμάρκετ;

where is the market?
poo **ee**ne ee laee**kee** agho**ra**
πού είναι η λαϊκή αγορά;

when is the market?
pote e**khee** laee**kee** agho**ra**
πότε έχει λαϊκή αγορά;

it's me next
ekho s**ee**ra
έχω σειρά

that's enough
ftanee
φτάνει

4 cakes
teserees **pa**stes
τέσσερις πάστες

a loaf of bread
ena pso**mee**
ένα ψωμί

a litre of...
ena **lee**tro...
ένα λίτρο...

milk
gha**la**
γάλα

wine
kra**see**
κρασί

olive oil
ele**o**ladho
ελαιόλαδο

a bottle of...
ena boo**ka**lee...
ένα μπουκάλι...

water
ne**ro**
νερό

sparkling
aery**oo**kho
αεριούχο

still
mee aery**oo**kho
μη αεριούχο

a can of...
ena koo**tee**...
ένα κουτί...

beer
beera
μπίρα

coke
coca **co**la
κόκα κόλα

orangeade
portoka**la**dha
πορτοκαλάδα

250 g of...
ena tetarto...
ένα τέταρτο...

taramosalata
taramosalata
ταραμοσαλάτα

cheese
teeree
τυρί

ham
zambon
ζαμπόν

butter
vooteero
βούτυρο

half a kilo of...
meeso kilo
μισό κιλό

tomatoes
domates
ντομάτες

green beans
fasolakya
φασολάκια

a kilo of...
ena keelo...
ένα κιλό...

potatoes
patates
πατάτες

apples
meela
μήλα

two cheese pies
dheeo teeropeetes
δύο τυρόπιτες

three spinach pies
trees spanakopeetes
τρεις σπανακόπιτες

a portion of...
meea mereedha...
μία μερίδα...

meat balls
keftedhes
κεφτέδες

macaroni
pasteetseeo
παστίτσιο

a packet of...
ena paketo...
ένα πακέτο...

biscuits
beeskota
μπισκότα

sugar
zakharee
ζάχαρη

a tin of...
ena kootee...
ένα κουτί...

tomatoes
domates
ντομάτες

mushrooms
maneetareea
μανιτάρια

a jar of...
ena dhokheeo...
ένα δοχείο...

honey
melee
μέλι

olives
elyes
ελιές

tee tha thelate
τι θα θέλατε;
can I help you?

katee allo
κάτι άλλο;
anything else?

SIGHTSEEING

ΤΟΥΡΙΣΤΙΚΟ ΓΡΑΦΕΙΟ	TOURIST OFFICE
ΕΟΤ	GREEK TOURIST OFFICE

Local tourist offices can provide free maps, help with booking accommodation, and advise on attractions and excursions. Museum opening hours are very variable so it is best to check before you visit. Monasteries open early in the morning and usually close at noon for three or four hours, opening again from about 4–7pm. Visitors should observe a strict dress code in both Greece and Cyprus: skirts and shorts should be below the knee.

where is the tourist office?
*poo **ee**ne to tooreesteek**o** ghraf**ee**o*
πού είναι το τουριστικό γραφείο;

we want to visit...
*th**e**loome na epeeskeft**oo**me...*
θέλουμε να επισκεφτούμε...

have you any leaflets?
*ekhete odheey**ee**es*
έχετε οδηγίες;

do you have a town guide?
*ekhete odheegh**o** tees p**o**lees*
έχετε οδηγό της πόλης;

in English
*sta angleek**a***
στα αγγλικά

we want to go to...
*th**e**loome na p**a**me sto / stee...*
θέλουμε να πάμε στο / στη...

are there any excursions?
*eep**a**rkhoon orghanees**me**nes ekdhrom**e**s*
υπάρχουν οργανομένες εκδρομές;

when does it leave?
*p**o**te f**e**vghoon*
πότε φεύγουν;

where does it leave from?
*ap**o** poo f**e**vghoon*
από που φεύγουν;

how much is it to get in?
*p**o**so kost**ee**zee ee seemetokh**ee***
πόσο κοστίζει η συμμετοχή;

is it open to the public?
*eene aneekt**o** sto keen**o***
είναι ανοικτό στο κοινό;

32

BEACH

ΑΠΑΓΟΡΕΥΤΕ Η ΚΟΛΥΜΒΗΣΗ	NO SWIMMING
ΑΠΑΓΟΡΕΥΤΕ Η ΚΑΤΑΔΥΣΗ	NO DIVING
ΠΡΟΣΟΧΗ ΚΙΝΔΥΝΟΣ	DANGER

At popular beaches you may be able to hire cabins, beach
umbrellas and deck chairs. Many have a bar on site and are
patrolled by a lifeguard (ναυαγοσώστης – navaghosostees) Signs
show where it is unsafe to swim. Many beach resorts have
facilities for watersports.

can you recommend a quiet beach?
kserete kapya eeseekhee paraleea
ξέρετε κάποια ήσυχη παραλία;

is there a pool?
ekhee peeseena
έχει πισίνα;

can we use the swimming pool?
boroome na khreeseemopyeesoome teen peeseena
μπορούμε να χρησιμοποιήσουμε την πισίνα;

can we swim in the lake?
boroome na koleembeesoome stee leemnee
μπορούμε να κολυμπήσουμε στη λίμνη;

is the water deep?
eene vathya
είναι βαθιά;

is the water clean?
eene to nero katharo
είναι το νερό καθαρό;

is it dangerous?
eene epeekeendheeno
είναι επικίνδυνο;

are there currents?
meepos ekhee revmata
μήπως έχει ρεύματα;

where can we...?
poo boroome na...
πού μπορούμε να...;

hire a beach umbrella
neekyasoome meea ombrela thalassees
νοικιάσουμε μία ομπρέλλα θαλάσσης;

windsurf
kanoome windsurfing
κάνουμε windsurfing

waterski
kanoome thalaseeo skee
κάνουμε θαλάσσιο σκι

SPORT

Most tourist offices have information on local sports facilities.

where can we...?
poo boroome na...
πού μπορούμε να...;

play tennis
peksoome tennis
παίξουμε τέννις

play golf
peksoome golf
παίξουμε γκολφ

hire bikes
neekyasoome podheelata
νοικιάσουμε ποδήλατα

go fishing
psarepsoome
ψαρέψουμε

go riding
kanoome eepaseea
κάνουμε ιππασία

how much is it...?
poso kosteezee...
πόσο κοστίζει...;

per hour
teen ora
την ώρα

per day
tee mera
τη μέρα

how do I book a court?
pos tha kano krateesee yeepedoo
πώς θα κάνω κράτηση γηπέδου;

do I need a fishing permit?
prepee na ekho adheea psarematos
πρέπει να έχω άδεια ψαρέματος;

can I hire...?
boro na neekyaso...
μπορώ να νοικιάσω...;

raquets
raketes
ρακέτες

golf clubs
bastooneea too golf
μπαστούνια του γκολφ

is there a football match?
ekhee podhosfereeko aghona
έχει ποδοσφαιρικό αγώνα;

who is playing
pyos pezee
ποιος παίζει;

where is there a sports shop?
poo eene ena katasteema me eedhee athleeteeka
πού είναι ένα κατάστημα με είδη αθλητικά;

Surprisingly enough, there are ski resorts in both Greece and Cyprus. In Greece they are at the Parnassus near Delphi but also in Epirus and the north of Greece. In Cyprus skiing is possible in the Troodos region.

can I hire skis?
boro na neekyaso skee
μπορώ να νοικιάσω σκι;

how much is a pass?
poso kosteezee ee karta teen eemera
πόσο κοστίζει η κάρτα την ημέρα;

I'm a beginner
eeme arkhareeos
είμαι αρχάριος

which is an easy run?
pyes eene efkoles dheeadhromes
ποιες είναι εύκολες διαδρομές;

what is the snow like today?
pos eene to khyonee seemera
πώς είναι το χιόνι σήμερα;

is there a map of the ski runs?
eeparkhee khartees me tees dheeadhromes
υπάρχει χάρτης με τις διαδρομές;

my skis are...
ta skee moo eene...
τα σκι μου είναι...

too long
polee makreea
πολύ μακριά

too short
polee konda
πολύ κοντά

my bindings are...
ee seendhesmee eene...
οι σύνδεσμοι είναι...

too loose
khalaree
χαλαροί

too tight
polee sfeekhtee
πολύ σφιχτοί

tee noomero eene ee botes sas
τι νούμερο είναι οι μπότες σας;
what is your boot size?

eeparkhee keendheenos khyonosteevadhas
υπάρχει κίνδυνος χιονοστιβάδας
there is danger of avalanches

NIGHTLIFE – popular

A list of cultural events is available in English-language newspapers inGreece. There are also special weekly publications listing entertainment for the whole week, often including a list of bars and restaurants for every taste. Note that the price you pay to get into clubs in Greece normally includes the cost of your first drink.

what can we do tonight?
tee tha kanoome apopse
τι θα κάνουμε απόψε;

which is a good bar?
pyo bar eene kalo
ποιο μπαρ είναι καλό;

is it in a safe area?
eene se asfalee pereeokhee
είναι σε ασφαλή περιοχή;

which is a good disco?
pya deeskotek eene kalee
ποια ντισκοτέκ είναι καλή;

is it expensive?
eene akreevee
είναι ακριβή;

where do local people go at night?
poo seeneetheesoon na dheeaskedhazoon ee dopyee ta vradhya
πού συνηθίζουν να διασκεδάζουν οι ντοπιοί τα βράδυα;

are there any concerts?
ekhee kapya seenavleea
έχει κάποια συναυλία;

no thanks, I don't want to
efkhareesto dhen thelo
ευχαριστώ, δεν θέλω

thelees na khorepsees
θέλεις να χορέψεις;
do you want to dance?

apo poo eese
από που είσαι;
where are you from?

pos se lene
πώς σε λένε;
what's your name?

me lene yorgos
με λένε Γιώργο
I'm Giorgos

If you are in Greece during the summer, ask about local festivals or fairs. And if you are in Athens, try not to miss the Athens festival from June to early September which takes place in beautiful locations such as the Theatre of Herodes Atticus at the foot of the Acropolis and the ancient theatre of Epidauros.

is there a list of cultural events?
eeparkhee meea leesta me tees ekdheelosees
υπάρχει μία λίστα με τις εκδηλώσεις;

are there any local festivals?
ekhee kapyo topeeko festival afteen teen pereeodho
έχει κάποιο τοπικό φεστιβίλ αυτήν την περίοδο;

we'd like to go...
tha thelame na pame...
θα θέλαμε να πάμε...;

to the theatre
sto theatro
στο θέατρο

to a concert
se meea seenavleea
σε μία συναυλία

to a performance in an ancient theatre
se meea parastasee se arkheeo theatro
σε μία παράσταση σε αρχαίο θέατρο

what's on?
tee ekdheelosees eeparkhoon
τι εκδηλώσεις υπάρχουν;

how much are the tickets?
poso kosteezoon ta eeseeteereea
πόσο κοστίζουν τα εισιτήρια;

do I need to book?
khreeazete na kleeso eeseeteereea
χρειάζεται να κλείσω εισιτήρια;

2 tickets...
dheeo eeseeteereea...
δύο εισιτήρια...

for tonight
ya apopse
για απόψε

for tomorrow night
ya avreeo
για αύριο

when does the performance end?
pote telyonee ee parastasee
πότε τελειώνει η παράσταση;

HOTEL

Tourist offices will be able to give you information on accommodation and help you make a booking. Accommodation in private homes does not exist in Cyprus.

have you a room for tonight?
ekhete ena dhomateeo ya apopse
έχετε ένα δωμάτιο για απόψε;

a single room
ena mono dhomateeo
ένα μονό δωμάτιο

a double room
ena dheeplo dhomateeo
ένα διπλό δωμάτιο

a family room
ena dhomateeo ya eekoyenya
ένα δωμάτιο για οικογένεια

with bathroom
me banyo
με μπάνιο

with shower
me doos
με ντους

how much is it?
poso kosteezee
πόσο κοστίζει;

is breakfast included?
to proeeno eene steen teemee
το πρωινό είναι στην τιμή;

I booked a room
ekho kanee meea krateesee
έχω κάνει μία κράτηση

my name is...
to onoma moo eene...
το όνομά μου είναι...

I'd like to see the room
tha eethela na dho to dhomateeo
θα ήθελα να δω το δωμάτιο

is there anything cheaper?
ekhete teepota ftheenotero
έχετε τίποτα φθηνότερο;

what time is...?
tee ora serveerete...
τι ώρα σερβίρεται...;

breakfast
to proeeno
το πρωινό

dinner
to vradheeno
το βραδυνό

we'll be back late tonight
tha epeestrepsoome argha apopse
θα επιστρέψουμε αργά απόψε

the key, please
to kleedhee, parakalo
το κλειδί, παρακαλώ

can you keep these in the safe?
boreete na krateesete afta sto khreematakeevotyo
μπορείτε να κρατήσετε αυτά στο χρηματακιβώτιο;

come in!
peraste
περάστε

please come back later
parakalo elate arghotera
παρακαλώ ελάτε αργότερα

can we have breakfast in our room?
boroome na paroome proeeno sto dhomateeo
μπορούμε να πάρουμε πρωινό στο δωμάτιο;

please bring...
parakalo na ferete...
παρακαλώ να φέρετε...

ashtray
ena tasakee
ένα τασάκι

soap
ena sapoonec
ένα σαπούνι

towels
petsetes
πετσέτες

a glass
ena poteeree
ένα ποτήρι

please clean...
parakalo na kathareesete...
παρακαλώ να καθαρίσετε...

my room
to dhomateeo moo
το δωμάτιο μου

the bathroom
to banyo
το μπάνιο

I would like a wake-up call...
tha eethela ena teelefoneema na kseepneeso...
θα ήθελα ένα τηλεφώνημα να ξυπνήσω...

at 7 o'clock
stees epta
στις επτά

is there a laundry service in the hotel?
ekhee pleendeereeo to ksenodhokheeo
έχει πλυντήριο το ξενοδοχείο;

I'm leaving tomorrow
fevgho avreeo
φεύγω αύριο

please prepare the bill
parakalo eteemasete to logharyasmo
παρακαλώ ετοιμάσετε το λογαριασμό

SELF-CATERING

The voltage in Greece is 220 V. If you plan to take any electrical appliances, such as an electric kettle or hairdryer, make sure you have an adaptor for the plug. The voltage in Cyprus is 240 V.

which is the key for this door?
*pyo **ee**ne to kleedh**ee** yee aft**ee**n teen p**o**rta*
ποιο είναι το κλειδί γι' αυτήν την πόρτα;

where are the fuses?
*poo **e**khee pr**ee**zes*
πού έχει πρίζες;

can you show me how this works?
*bor**ee**te na moo dh**ee**ksete pos leetoory**ee***
μπορείτε να μου δείξετε πώς λειτουργεί;

how does ... work?	**the dishwasher**	**the cooker**
*pos leetoory**ee**...*	*to pleend**ee**reeo py**a**ton*	*ee kooz**ee**na*
πώς λειτουργεί...;	το πλυντήριο πιάτων	η κουζίνα
	the washing machine	**the waterheater**
	*to pleend**ee**reeo*	*o thermos**ee**fonas*
	το πλυντήριο	ο θερμοσήφωνας

who do I speak to if there are any problems?
*se pyon apevthee**n**tho an eep**a**rkhee k**a**pyo pr**o**vleema*
σε ποιόν απευθυνθώ αν υπάρχει κάποιο πρόβλημα;

where do I put the rubbish?
*poo pet**a**me ta skoop**ee**dhya*
πού πετάμε τα σκουπίδια;

the gas has run out
*ee fy**a**lee too gazy**oo** tel**ee**ose*
η φιάλη του γκαζιού τελείωσε

what do I do?
*tee na k**a**no*
τι να κάνω;

CAMPING & CARAVANNING

Free camping in Greece is now illegal and carries the risk of a heavy fine. The tourist office can help you to find suitable campsites. There are six campsites on Cyprus.

we're looking for a campsite
psakhnoome ya thesee kamping
ψάχνουμε για θέση κάμπινγκ

have you a list of campsites?
ekhete leesta me ta kamping
έχετε λίστα με τα κάμπινγκ;

have you any vacancies?
ekhete thesees
έχετε θέσεις;

how much is it per night?
poso kosteezee ee vradya
πόσο κοστίζει η βραδυά;

how far is the beach?
poso makreea eene ee paraleea
πόσο μακριά είναι η παραλία;

we'd like to stay for ... nights
theloome na meenoome ... vradya
θέλουμε να μείνουμε ... βράδυα

is the campsite sheltered?
ekhete thesees me skepastro
έχετε θέσεις με σκέπαστρο;

can we have a more sheltered site?
boroome na ekhoome meea thesee me skepastro
μπορούμε να έχουμε μία θέση με σκέπαστρο;

this site is very muddy
aftee ee thesee eene ekhee laspee
αυτή η θέση είναι έχει λάσπη

is there another site?
ekhete kamya alee
έχετε καμμιά άλλη;

can we park our caravan here overnight?
boroome na afeesoome to trokhospeeto mas edho teen neekhta
μπορούμε να αφήσουμε το τροχοσπιτό μας εδώ την νύχτα;

can we put our tent here?
boroome na steesoome edho teen skeenee mas
μπορούμε να στήσουμε εδώ την σκηνή μας;

CHILDREN

a child's ticket
ena pedheeko eeseeteereeo
ένα παιδικό εισητήριο

he/she is ... years old
eene ... khronon
είναι ... χρονών

is there a reduction for children?
eeparkhee eedheekee teemee ya pedya
υπάρχει ειδική τιμή για παιδιά;

is there a children's menu?
eeparkhee pedheeko menoo
υπάρχει παιδικό μενού;

have you...?	**a high chair**	**a cot**
ekhete...	*meea pedheekee karekla*	*ena pedheeko krevatee*
έχετε...;	μία παιδική καρέκλα	ένα παιδικό κρεββάτι;

is it ok to bring children?
eeparkhee provleema an feroome ta pedhya
υπάρχει πρόβλημα αν φέρουμε τα παιδιά;

what is there for children to do?
tee boroon na kanoon ta pedhya
τι μπορούν να κάνουν τα παιδιά;

where is a play park?
poo eene ee pedheekee khara
πού είναι η παιδική χαρά;

I have lost...	**my child**	**my children**
ekhasa...	*to pedhee moo*	*ta pedhya moo*
έχασα...	το παιδί μου	τα παιδιά μου

is it safe for children?
eene asfales ya ta pedhya
είναι ασφαλές για τα παιδιά;

is it dangerous
eene epeekeendheeno
είναι επικίνδυνο;

I have two children
ekho dheeo pedhya
έχω δύο παιδιά

do you have children?
ekhete pedhya
έχετε παιδιά;

SPECIAL NEEDS

Provision for the disabled has been low in the past but is gradually improving. Some churches and museums will have access ramps or lifts, but many do not. Most Intercity trains now have facilities for the disabled.

is it possible to visit ... with a wheelchair?
eene dheenato na epeeskeftoome ... me anapeereeko karotsakee
είναι δυνατό να επισκευφτούμε ... με αναπηρικό καροτσάκι;

do you have toilets for the disabled?
ekhete tooaletes ya anapeeroos
έχετε τουαλέτες για αναπήρους;

I need a bedroom on the ground floor
khreeazome eepnodhomateeo sto eesoyeeo
χρειάζομαι υπνοδωμάτιο στο ισόγειο

is there a lift?
ekhee asanser
έχει ασανσέρ;

where is the lift?
poo eene to asanser
πού είναι το ασανσέρ;

are there many steps?
ekhee pola skalya
έχει πολλά σκαλιά;

is there an entrance for wheelchairs?
eeparkhee eedheekee eesodho ya anapeereeko karotsakee
υπάρχει ειδική είσοδο για αναπηρικό καροτσάκι;

is there a place on this train for a wheelchair?
eeparkhee thesee sto treno ya anapeereeko karotsakee
υπάρχει θέση στο τρένο για αναπηρικό καροτσάκι;

is there a reduction for the disabled?
eeparkhee eedheekee teemee ya anapeeroos
υπάρχει ειδική τιμή για αναπήρους;

EXCHANGE VISITORS

These phrases are intended for families hosting Greek-speaking visitors. We have used the informal form for these phrases.

did you sleep well?
keemeetheekes kala
κοιμήθηκες καλά;

would you like to take a shower?
thelees na kanees ena doos
θέλεις να κάνεις ένα ντους;

what would you like for breakfast?
tee tha eetheles ya proeeno
τι θα ήθελες για πρωινό;

do you eat...?
tros...
τρως...;

what would you like to eat / drink?
tee thelees na pyees / fas
τι θέλεις να πιείς / φας;

do you drink...?
peenees...
πίνεις...;

what would you like to do today?
pos thelees na perasees teen eemera
πώς θέλεις να περάσεις την ημέρα;

would you like to go shopping?
thelees na pame ya psonya
θέλεις να πάμε για ψώνια;

I will pick you up at...
tha peraso na se paro stees...
θα περάσω να σε πάρω στις...

did you enjoy yourself?
perases kala
πέρασες καλά;

take care
na prosekhees
να προσέχεις

please be back by...
an thelees na epeestrepsees stees...
αν θέλεις να επιστρέψεις στις...

we'll be in bed when you get back
tha ekhoome paee ya eepno otan tha epeestrepsees
θα έχουμε πάει για ύπνο όταν θα επιστρέψεις

EXCHANGE VISITORS

These phrases are intended for those people staying with Greek-speaking families. We have used the formal form for these phrases.

I like...
moo aresee...
μου αρέσει...

I don't like...
dhen moo aresee...
δεν μου αρέσει...

that was delicious
eetan nosteemo
ήταν νόστιμο

may I phone home?
boro na teelefoneeso sto speetee
μπορώ να τηλεφωνίσω στο σπίτι;

can I have a key?
boro na ekho ena kleedhee
μπορώ να έχω ένα κλειδί;

can you take me by car?
boreete na me pate me to aftokeeneeto
μπορείτε να με πάτε με το αυτοκίνητο;

can I borrow...?
boro na dhaneeso...
μπορώ να δανείσω...;

an iron
to seedhero
το σίδερο

a hairdryer
to peestolakee
το πιστολάκι

what time do I have to get up?
tee ora prepee na kseepneeso
τι ώρα πρέπει να ξυπνήσω;

please would you call me at...?
boreete na moo teelefoneesete stees
μπορείτε να μου τηλεφωνίσετε στις...;

how long are you staying?
poson kero tha menete
πόσον καιρό θα μένετε;

I'm leaving in a week
fevgho se meea evdhomadha
φεύγω σε μία εβδομάδα

thanks for everything
efkhareesto ya ola
ευχαριστώ για όλα

I've had a great time
perasa para polee oreea
πέρασα πάρα πολύ ωραία

PROBLEMS

can you help me?
boreete na me voeetheesete
μπορείτε να με βοηθήσετε;

I don't speak Greek
dhen meelao eleeneeka
δεν μιλάω Ελληνικά

do you speak English?
meelate angleeka
μιλάτε Αγγλικά;

does anyone speak English?
meelaee kapyos angleeka
μιλάει κάποιος Αγγλικά;

I'm lost
ekho khathee
έχω χαθεί

how do I get to...?
pos boro na pao sto / stee...
πώς μπορώ να πάω στο / στη...;

I'm late
ekho aryeesee
έχω αργήσει

I need to get to...
prepee na pao sto / stee...
πρέπει να πάω στο / στη...

I've missed...
ekhasa...
έχασα...

my plane
to aeroplano
το αεροπλάνο

my connection
teen andapokreesee moo
την ανταπόκρισή μου

I've lost...
ekhasa...
έχασα...

my money
ta lefta moo
τα λεφτά μου

my passport
to dheeavateereeo moo
το διαβατήριό μου

my camera
tee fotoghrafeekee meekhanee moo
τη φωτογραφική μηχανή μου

my keys
ta kleedhya moo
τα κλειδιά μου

my suitcase isn't here
ee valeetsa moo dhen eene edho
η βαλίτσα μου δεν είναι εδώ

I have no money
dhen ekho lefta
δεν έχω λεφτά

I've left my bag in...
ksekhasa teen tsanda moo...
ξέχασα την τσάντα μου...

on the coach
sto leoforeeo
στο λεωφορείο

leave me alone! *(female)*
afeese me eeseekhee
άφησέ με ήσυχη

go away!
feeye
φύγε

46

COMPLAINTS

the light
to fos
το φως

the toilet
ee tooaleta
η τουαλέτα

the telephone
to teelefono
το τηλέφωνο

the heating
ee thermansee
η θέρμανση

...doesn't work
...dhen leetooryee
...δεν λειτουργεί

the room is dirty
to dhomateeo eene vromeeko
το δωμάτιο είναι βρώμικο

I don't like the room
dhen moo aresee to dhomateeo
δεν μου αρέσει το δωμάτιο

I didn't order this
dhen zeeteesa afto
δεν ζήτησα αυτό

I want to complain
thelo na kano parapona
θέλω να κάνω παράπονα

I want a refund
thelo ta lefta moo peeso
θέλω τα λεφτά μου πίσω

the bath is dirty
to banyo eene vromeeko
το μπάνιο είναι βρώμικο

it's too noisy
ekhee polee thoreevo
έχει πολύ θόρυβο

we've been waiting for a very long time
pereemenoome polee ora
περιμένουμε πολλή ώρα

we're in a hurry
eemaste vyasteekee
είμαστε βιαστικοί

this is broken
afto eene khalasmeno
αυτό είναι χαλασμένο

there is a mistake
ekhete kanee lathos
έχετε κάνει λάθος

can you repair it?
boreete na to epeedheeorthosete
μπορείτε να το επιδιορθώσετε;

EMERGENCIES

ΕΛΛΗΝΙΚΗ ΑΣΤΥΝΟΜΙΑ	POLICE
ΠΥΡΟΣΒΕΣΤΙΚΗ	FIRE BRIGADE
ΕΠΕΙΓΟΝΤΑ ΠΕΡΙΣΤΑΤΙΚΑ	CASUALTY DEPARTMENT

To call an emergency ambulance, dial **166** and report the emergency along with your name and location.
The number for the fire brigade is **199**.

help!
voeetheea
βοήθεια

can you help me?
boreete na me voeetheesete
μπορείτε να με βοηθήσετε;

there's been an accident
ekhee yeenee ateekheema
έχει γίνει ατύχημα

someone is injured
eeparkhoon travmatees
υπάρχουν τραυματίες

please call...
parakalo kaleste...
παρακαλώ καλέστε...

the police
teen asteenomeea
την αστυνομία

an ambulance
ena asthenoforo
ένα ασθενοφόρο

he was going too fast
etrekhe me meghalee takheeteeta
έτρεχε με μεγάλη ταχύτητα

that man keeps following me
ekeenos o andras me akoloothee seenekhos
εκείνος ο άντρας με ακολουθεί συνεχώς

where's the police station?
poo eene to asteenomeeko tmeema
πού είναι το αστυνομικό τμήμα;

I want to report a theft
thelo na dheeloso meea klopee
θέλω να δηλώσω μία κλοπή

I've been robbed
ekho pesee theema klopees
έχω πέσει θύμα κλοπής

I've been attacked
ekho pesee theema efodhoo klepton
έχω πέσει θύμα εφόδου κλεπτών

my car has been broken into
paraveeasan to aftokeeneeto moo
παραβίασαν το αυτοκίνητό μου

my car has been stolen
eklepsan to aftokeeneeto moo
έκλεψαν το αυτοκίνητό μου

I've been raped
me veeasan
με βίασαν

I need a report for my insurance
khreeazome khartee pereeghrafees seemvandon ya teen asfaleea moo
χρειάζομαι χαρτί περιγραφής συμβάντων για την ασφάλεια μου

how much is the fine?
poso eene to prosteemo
πόσο είναι το προστιμό;

where do I pay it?
poo boro na to pleeroso
πού μπορώ να το πληρώσω;

I would like to phone the British Consulate
thelo na teelefoneeso sto vretaneeko prokseneeo
θέλω να τηλεφωνίσω στο βρετανικό προξενείο

I have no money
dhen ekho lefta
δεν έχω λεφτά

---

erkhomaste amesos
ερχόμαστε αμέσως
we're on our way

HEALTH

ΦΑΡΜΑΚΕΙΟ	PHARMACY
ΝΟΣΟΚΟΜΕΙΟ	HOSPITAL
ΕΠΕΙΓΟΝΤΑ ΠΕΡΙΣΤΑΤΙΚΑ	CASUALTY DEPARTMENT

EU citizens are entitled to free emergency care in Greece. You should take with you form E111, completed and stamped at a post office in the UK before your trip. However you will need to take out a medical insurance policy to cover non-emergency treatment.

have you something for...?
moo dheenete katee ya...
μου δίνετε κάτι για...;

car sickness
zalee sto aftokeeneeto
ζάλη στο αυτοκίνητο

diarrhoea
dheeareea
διάρροια

is it safe to give children?
eene asfales ya ta pedhya
είναι ασφαλές για τα παιδιά;

I feel ill
dhen esthanome kala
δεν αισθάνομαι καλά

I need a doctor
khreeazome yatro
χρειάζομαι γιατρό

my son is ill
o yos moo eene arostos
ο γιος μου είναι άρρωστος

my daughter is ill
ee koree moo eene arostee
η κόρη μου είναι άρρωστη

I'm on this medication
perno afta ta farmaka
παίρνω αυτά τα φάρμακα

I have high blood pressure
ekho eepertasee
έχω υπέρταση

I'm diabetic *(m/f)*
eeme dheeaveeteekos/ee
είμαι διαβητικός/ή

I'm pregnant
eeme engeeos
είμαι έγγυος

I'm on the pill
perno anteeseeleepteeka
παίρνω αντισυλληπτικά

50

I'm allergic to penicillin
ekho aleryeea steen peneekeeleenee
έχω αλλεργία στην πενικιλλίνη

my blood group is...
ekho omadha ematos...
έχω ομάδα αίματος...

I'm breastfeeding
theelazo to moro moo
θηλάζω το μωρό μου

is it safe to take?
eene asfales kata teen ghalookheea
είναι ασφαλές κατά την γαλουχία;

will he/she have to go to hospital?
prepee na bee sto nosokomeeo
πρέπει να μπει στο νοσοκομείο;

where is the hospital?
poo eene to nosokomeeo
πού είναι το νοσοκομείο;

I need to go to casualty
prepee na pao sta epeeghonda pereestateeka
πρέπει να πάω στα επείγοντα περιστατικά

when are visiting hours?
pote ekhee epeeskepteereeo
πότε έχει επισκεπτήριο;

which ward?
pya kleeneekee
ποια κλινική;

I need a dentist
khreeazome odhondyatro
χρειάζομαι οδοντιατρό

I have toothache
ekho ponodhondo
έχω πονόδοντο

the filling has come out
moo efeeye to sfrayeesma
μου έφυγε το σφράγισμα

do I have to pay now?
prepee na pleeroso tora
πρέπει να πληρώσω τώρα;

I have an abscess in the tooth
ekho ena aposteema sto dondee
έχω ένα απόστημα στο δόντι

it hurts
me ponaee
με πονάει

can you repair my dentures?
boreete na moo epeedheeorthosete teen odhondosteekheea
μπορείτε να μου επιδιορθώσετε την οδοντοστοιχία;

BUSINESS

Public offices open from 8am–3pm. Private companies usually work from 8am–5pm or even 7pm.

here's my card
krateeste teen karta moo
κρατήστε την κάρτα μου

I'm from the Smith Company
eeme apo teen etereea Smith
είμαι από την εταιρία Smith

I want to make an appointment
tha eethela ena randevoo
θα ήθελα ένα ραντεβού

with Mr/Ms...
me ton keereeo /teen keereea...
με τον κύριο / την κυρία...

for April 4th at 11 o'clock
ya tees teserees apreeleeoo stees endeka to proee
για τις τέσσερις Απριλίου στις έντεκα το πρωί

can we meet at a restaurant?
boroome na seenandeethoome se ena esteeatoreeo ya fayeeto
μπορούμε να συναντηθούμε σε ένα εστιατόριο για φαγητό;

I will send a fax to confirm
tha steelo ena fax ya na epeeveveoso teen eemera ke ora
θα στείλω ένα φαξ για να επιβεβαιώσω την ημέρα και ώρα

I'm staying at Hotel...
meno sto ksenodhokheeo...
μένω στο ξενοδοχείο...

how do I get to your office?
pos boro na ertho sto ghrafeeo sas
πώς μπορώ να έρθω στο γραφείο σας;

here is some information about my company
krateeste mereekes pleeroforeeyes ya teen etereea moo
κρατήστε μερικές πληροφορίες για την εταιρεία μου

BUSINESS

I have an appointment with...
ekho randevoo me ton / teen...
έχω ραντεβού με τον / την...

at ... o'clock
stees...
στις...

delighted to meet you!
khero polee
χαίρω πολύ

my Greek isn't very good
ta eleeneeka moo dhen eene polee kala
τα ελληνικά μου δεν είναι πολύ καλά

what is the name of the managing director
pos leyete o dhee-evtheentees
πώς λέγεται ο διευθυντής

I would like some information about your company
tha eethela mereekes pleeroforeeyes ya teen etereea sas
θα ήθελα μερικές πληροφορίες για την εταιρεία σας

do you have a press office?
ekhete tmeema teepoo
έχετε τμήμα τύπου;

I need an interpreter
khreeazome ena dhee-ermeenea
χρειάζομαι ένα διερμηνέα

can you photocopy this for me?
boreete na fototeepeesete afto
μπορείτε να φωτοτυπήσετε αυτό;

where is the conference room?
poo eene ee ethoosa seeskepseon
πού είναι η αίθουσα συσκέψεων;

ekhete randevoo έχετε ραντεβού; do you have an appointment?	*tee ora* τι ώρα; at what time?

PHONING

Coin-operated local call phone boxes take 50 drachmas. However card-operated machines are much more common – you can buy phonecards in Greece for 100, 500 and 1,000 units. To call the UK, dial 00 44 then the area code without the first 0.

a phonecard
meea teelekarta
μία τηλεκάρτα

I want to make a phone call
thelo na kano ena teelefoneema
θέλω να κάνω ένα τηλεφώνημα

Mr Raptis, please
ton keereeo Raptee parakalo
τον κύριο Ραπτη, παρακαλώ

extension ..., please
esotereeko ... parakalo
εσωτερικό ... παρακαλώ

can I speak to...?
boro na meeleeso ston / steen...
μπορώ να μιλήσω στον / στην...;

this is Jim Brown
Jim Brown edho
Jim Brown εδώ

I'll call back later
tha teelefoneeso arghotera
θα τηλεφωνήσω αργότερα

I'll call back tomorrow
tha ksanateelefoneeso avreeo
θα ξανατηλεφωνήσω αύριο

can I have an outside line, please
boro na ekho meea eksotereeko ghrammee parakalo
μπορώ να έχω μία εξωτερικό γραμμή, παρακαλώ

do you have a mobile?
ekhete keeneeto
έχετε κινητό;

what is the number?
pyo eene to noomero
ποιο είναι το νούμερο;

where can I recharge my mobile phone?
poo boro na forteeso to keeneeto moo
πού μπορώ να φορτίσω το κινητό μου;

---

leyete
λέγεται
hello

pyos eene
ποιος είναι;
who is calling?

meelaee
μιλάει
it's engaged

boreete na teelefoneesete arghotera
μπορείτε να τηλεφωνήσετε αργότερα;
can you call back later?

FAXING/E-MAIL

I want to send a fax
thelo na steelo ena fax
θέλω να στείλω ένα φαξ

do you have a fax?
ekhete fax
έχετε φαξ;

what's your fax number?
pyo eene to noomero too fax sas
ποιο είναι το νούμερο του φαξ σας;

please resend your fax
parakalo ksanasteelte to fax sas
παρακαλώ ξαναστείλτε το φαξ σας

I can't read it
dhen boro na to dheeavaso
δεν μπορώ να το διαβάσω

your fax is constantly engaged
to fax sas eene seenekhos kateeleemeno
το φαξ σας είναι συνεχώς κατειλημένο

where can I send a fax from?
poo boro na steelo ena fax
πού μπορώ να στείλω ένα φαξ;

did you get my fax?
lavate to fax moo
λάβατε το φαξ μου;

I want to send an e-mail
thelo na steelo ena email
θέλω να στείλω ένα e-mail

what's your e-mail address?
pyo eene to email sas
ποιο είναι το e-mail σας;

did you get my e-mail?
peerate to email moo
πήρατε το e-mail μου;

to email moo eene...
το e-mail μου είναι...
my e-mail address is...

NUMBERS

0	μηδέν meedhen	1st	πρώτος protos
1	ένα ena		
2	δύο dheeo	2nd	δεύτερος dhevteros
3	τρία treea		
4	τέσσερα tesera	3rd	τρίτος treetos
5	πέντε pende		
6	έξι eksee	4th	τέταρτος tetartos
7	επτά epta		
8	οκτώ okto	5th	πέμπτος pemptos
9	εννέα enea		
10	δέκα dheka	6th	έκτος ektos
11	έντεκα endeka		
12	δώδεκα dhodheka	7th	εφτός eftos
13	δεκατρία dhekatreea		
14	δεκατέσσερα dhekatesera	8th	οκτός oktos
15	δεκαπέντε dhekapende		
16	δεκαέξι dhekaeksee	9th	εννάιος eneos
17	δεκαεφτά dhekaefta		
18	δεκαοκτώ dhekaokto	10th	δεκατός dhekatos
19	δεκαεννέα dhekaenea		
20	είκοσι eekosee		
21	είκοσι ένα eekosee ena		
22	είκοσι δύο eekosee dheeo		
30	τριάντα treeanda		
40	σαράντα saranda		
50	πενήντα peneenda		
60	εξήντα ekseenda		
70	εβδομήντα evdhomeenda		
80	ογδόντα oghdhonda		
90	ενενήντα eneneenda		
100	εκατό ekato		
110	εκατόν δέκα ekaton dheka		
500	πεντακόσια pendakosya		
1,000	χίλια kheelya		
2,000	δύο χιλιάδες dheeo kheeleeadhes		
1,000,000	ένα εκατομμύριο ena ekatomeereeo		

DAYS & MONTHS

Key words to look out for on timetables are **καθημερινές** (katheemereen**es**) meaning weekday (i.e. Mon–Sat) and **Κυριακές και γιορτές** (keereeyak**es** ke yort**es**) meaning Sundays and public holidays. Timetables vary according to whether they are **θερινές** (thereen**es** – summer) or **χειμερινές** (kheemereen**es** – winter).

Ιανουάριος	January			
Φεβρουάριος	February			
Μάρτιος	March	Δευτέρα	Monday
Απρίλιος	April	Τρίτη	Tuesday
Μαϊος	May	Τετάρτη	Wednesday
Ιούνιος	June	Πέμπτη	Thursday
Ιούλιος	July	Παρασκευή	Friday
Αύγουστος	August	Σάββατο	Saturday
Σεπτέμβριος	September	Κυριακή	Sunday
Οκτώβριος	October			
Νοέμβριος	November			
Δεκέμβριος	December			

what's the date?
tee eemeromeen**ee**a ekh**oo**me s**ee**mera
τι ημερομηνία έχουμε σήμερα;

which month?
pyos m**ee**nas
ποιός μήνας;

it's the 5th of March 2001
eene p**e**nde mart**ee**oo dh**ee**o kheelyadhes **e**na
είναι πέντε Μαρτίου δύο χιλιάδες ένα

on Saturday
to s**a**vato
το Σάββατο

on Saturdays
ta s**a**vata
τα Σάββατα

every Saturday
k**a**the s**a**vato
κάθε Σάββατο

next Saturday
to erkh**o**meno s**a**vato
το ερχόμενο Σάββατο

last Saturday
to proeegh**oo**meno s**a**vato
το προηγούμενο Σάββατο

TIME

Note that throughout Europe the 24-hour clock is used much more widely than in the UK.

excuse me, what time is it?
tee ora eene parakalo
τι ώρα είναι, παρακαλώ;

am
pro meseemvreeas
προ μεσημβρίας

pm
meta meseemvreeas
μετά μεσημβρίας

at midday
to meseemeree
το μεσημέρι

at midnight
ta mesaneekhta
τα μεσάνυχτα

it's 1 o'clock
eene meea ee ora
είναι μία η ώρα

it's six o'clock
eene eksee ee ora
είναι έξι η ώρα

it's 10 past 8
eene okto ke dheka
είναι οκτώ και δέκα

it's 10 to 8
eene okto para dheka
είναι οκτώ παρά δέκα

an hour
meea ora
μία ώρα

half an hour
meesee ora
μισή ώρα

until 8 o'clock
mekhree stees okto
μέχρι στις οκτώ

it is half past 8
eene okto ke meesee
είναι οκτώ και μισή

at 10 o'clock
stees dheka
στις δέκα

at 2200
stees dheka to vradhee
στις δέκα το βράδυ

soon
seendoma
σύντομα

later
arghotera
αργότερα

FOOD

ORDERING DRINKS

Although you may order different courses, you will find that they all tend to arrive at the same time. Food is generally lukewarm rather than hot. Any tips should be left on the table, the amount is up to you.

a coffee
ena neskafe
ένα νεσκαφέ

a Greek coffee
ena eleeneeko kafe
ένα ελληνικό καφέ

2 white coffees
dheeo kafedhes me ghala
δύο καφέδες με γάλα

a tea
ena tsaee
ένα τσάι

with milk
me ghala
με γάλα

with lemon
me lemonee
με λεμόνι

a lager
meea beera
μία μπίρα

small
mekree
μικρή

large
meghalee
μεγάλη

a bottle of mineral water
ena bookalee metaleeko nero
ένα μπουκάλι μεταλλικό νερό

sparkling
aeryookho
αεριούχο

still
mee aeryookho
μη αεριούχο

would you like a drink?
thelete katee na pyeete
θέλετε κάτι να πιείτε;

what will you have?
tee tha thelate
τι θα θέλατε;

the wine list, please
ton katalogho krasyon parakalo
τον κατάλογο κρασιών, παρακαλώ

a carafe of house wine
meea karafa krasee
μία καράφα κρασί

a glass of wine
ena poteeree krasee
ένα ποτήρι κρασί

a bottle of wine
ena bookalee krasee
ένα μπουκάλι κρασί

red
kokeeno
κόκκινο

white
lefko
λευκό

ORDERING FOOD

where is there a good local restaurant?
eeparkhee kapyo kalo esteeatoreeo edho
υπάρχει κάποιο καλό εστιατόριο εδώ;

I'd like to book a table
thelo na krateeso ena trapezee
θέλω να κρατήσω ένα τραπέζι

for ... people
ya ... atoma
για ... άτομα

for tonight
ya apopse
για απόψε

at 8 pm
ya tees okto to vradhee
για τις οκτώ το βράδυ

the menu, please
ton katalogho parakalo
τον κατάλογο, παρακαλώ

is there a dish of the day?
ekhee pyato tees eemeras
έχει πιάτο της ημέρας;

can we choose from the display?
boroome na dhoome tee ekhete
μπορούμε να δούμε τι έχετε;

I'll have this
tha paro afto
θα πάρω αυτό

what do you recommend?
tee proteenete
τι προτείνετε;

I don't eat meat
dhen tro-o kreas
δεν τρώω κρέας

do you have any vegetarian dishes?
ekhete katee ya khortofaghoos
έχετε κάτι για χορτοφάγους;

excuse me!
parakalo
παρακαλώ

please bring more...
fernete leegho...
φέρνετε λίγο...

bread
psomee
ψωμί

water
nero
νερό

the bill, please
to logharyasmo parakalo
το λογαριασμό παρακαλώ

kalee oreksee
καλή όρεξη
enjoy your meal!

GREEK FOOD

The immense diversity of the Greek landscape is abundantly reflected in the variety of food to be found both on the islands and on the mainland. When thinking of Greece one tends to visualize a vast archipelago spread out through the Aegean Sea and culminating with Crete, the largest and southernmost island. But we must not forget mainland Greece, with its mountainous north bordering several countries and its long, sinuous coastline.

A tumultuous past, chequered with invaders and conquerors – spanning thousands of years – has left a profound mark on the land and the people, touching all aspects of Greek life, from the arts to food. It was only quite recently in historical terms that the modern Greek state came into existence. Nevertheless the Greek way of life and traditional values were not lost and became the foundations for the new state.

Distinctive as each place is, there is a unifying theme found in Greek food and reflected in the unfussy, wholesome and healthy dishes, with the emphasis on local produce and the seasons.

Greeks like to eat out with their families and friends (al fresco, if the weather permits) so you will find that popular eating places are bustling with life.

The Greeks are arguably the best exponents of the currently fashionable 'Mediterranean diet'. They have a great liking for salads well-seasoned with plenty of olive oil and large platters of cooked vegetables swimming in the golden, precious liquid, which is the pride of the country.

Another food loved by all Greeks is the now famous and exceedingly good yoghurt (*yaoortee*) which they eat mixed liberally with honey (*melee*) for breakfast (if they have any breakfast at all). Many just take a small strong coffee (*kafes*) like an *espresso*. If you cannot face the morning without this first meal, head for the bakery (*foornos*), for some freshly baked ordinary bread (*psomee*) or wholemeal (*psomee oleekees aleseos*), to eat with cheese (*teeree*) or olives (*elyes*). The bakers also sell delicious cheese pies (*teeropeetes*) and various other savoury goods, as well as spicy and sweet biscuits (*booteemata*) which are good and filling. All these foods and many more are obtainable in the morning or you can order a Continental-style breakfast at café-cum-pâtisserie establishments called *ghalaktopol**eeo*** and *zakharoplast**eeo***, where they sell sweets and cakes as well as Greek coffee (*eleeneek**os** kaf**es***), instant coffee (*neskafe*), tea (*ts**aee***) and bread (*psom**ee***) with butter and honey (*m**elee ke v**oo**teero*) or jam (*marmel**adha*).

Any time is an appropriate time for eating in Greece and there are plenty of delicious snacks available throughout the day – you don't even have to set foot in a restaurant! Try toasted sandwiches (*s**andv**eets*), or gyros (*y**ee**ros*), pitta bread with a meat, tomato, onion and sauce filling.

Probably the most well-known of food traditions in the whole of Greece and Cyprus, and one that perhaps most characterizes the real taste of the country, is the famous *mez**edhes** – also known as *meze* or *mez**es** – which literally means 'mixture'. They are savoury titbits, such as olives, platters with salad, plus small portions of various dishes. They can constitute a meal in themselves but are generally served as a starter (or alternatively a snack). Some of the best now appear at new tourist-geared places called *oozer**ee** (serving ouzo). Eating a good variety of *mez**edhes* one can very quickly get an overall taste of Greek gastronomy.

THE REGIONS

The Athens area is undoubtedly the centre of the country. People from all over Greece have moved there and brought with them their culinary traditions. Hence one can find a huge diversity of cuisine. Around the capital agricultural land is rich in produce filling the Athens' markets. Try *souvlak**eea** (lamb or pork seasoned with herbs and barbecued on a skewer), for instance, from one of the many street vendors, or grilled chicken basted with olive oil (*kot**opoulo reegan**ato*), as well as the usual Greek favourites such as *dolm**adhes* (stuffed vine leaves). Sweets and chocolates are a temptation. Try the local halva (*chalv**as*, a sweetmeat made from sesame seeds) and fruit and nut cakes such as *boog**atsa*. Icecream and fruit are also well worth trying.

The Peloponnese is a beautiful region, with an abundance of crops to match – including vineyards, olive groves and figs. Here, like elsewhere

GREEK FOOD

in Greece, you will find hospitable people and simple, healthy food at reasonable prices. Grilled meats and snacks of every kind are available at the many tavernas, as well as the ubiquitous *mezedhes*. Along the coastline many tavernas specialize in seafood. Try also the traditional lamb dish, *arnee me votana* (a stew with herbs and vegetables). Dried figs in wine syrup are served as a dessert, with cheese (*seeka mavrodafnee*).

In central and western Greece, and especially in the fertile province of Thessaly, industry has taken a stronghold, but agriculture still plays a very important role as well. This region is visited mainly because of places like Delphi, the ancient oracle, or the monasteries at Meteora. Restaurants and tavernas in these areas are very reasonable. Look for *kokorestee*, a kebab speciality made with liver. Meat is actually a strong point on the menu, particularly when away from the sea. Casseroles are good and wholesome. In the Epirus area try the local *peetes*, a variety of meat or vegetable pies in different shapes and sizes. Around the coast seafood is, of course, abundant, with fish *mezedhes* popular, including grilled sardines (*sardheles*) and fried whitebait (*mareedha*). Wine is quite good and the traditional *oozeree*-type places worth visiting for their splendid *mezedhes*. A famous variety of the custard tart (*boogatsa*) originated in Ioannina. *Tseepooro* is a very strong spirit typical of Central Greece.

Northern Greece (Macedonia and Thrace) borders on the former Yugoslav Republic of Macedonia, Bulgaria and Turkey and naturally bears very strong influences from these countries. Walnuts and pickles are two of these influences. In Thessaloniki, especially, there is now an increasing number of eating places. Elsewhere tavernas are good value with the coast offering excellent seafood, although in the interior there is also good freshwater fish from the many lakes in this area. Try the local meatballs (*soutzoukakeea*) that are very spicy. Another meat dish worth trying is made with goat, lamb or even beef, cooked in a sauce until tender (*tas kebab*). Inland you can find very good *mezedhes* including smoked fish accompanied with a walnut sauce flavoured with garlic plus cracked olives (*skordhalya me psaree kapneesto*). Here, as in the rest of Greece, you will be served *pasatempo* (pumpkin seeds). For a dessert look out for filo pastries with nuts, honey and cinnamon, and prunes served with cream and a sweet wine sauce.

THE ISLANDS

The islands, too numerous to quote by name, are spread over a vast area and food is influenced by the abundance of their own produce or lack of it and the islands' history. All over Greece people depend and make the most of what is available locally, while keeping to the underlying traditions of, for example, *mezedhes*. The islands are naturally rich in seafood. Oysters (*streedhya*), crab (*kavooras*) and other sea delicacies are popular but don't miss other things, like *khtapodheea*, a salad made with squid or octopus in vinaigrette, the very popular fried mullet (*barboonee*), fresh grilled tuna (*tonos pseetos*) or baked seabass (*lavrakee*) with vegetables. Those islands which do possess grazing land will also have an abundance of meat dishes, such as lamb cutlets (*arnakee pseeto*). Try the special pasta and meat dish (*pasteetseeo*), also widely available on the mainland, which consists of macaroni layered with mincemeat and white sauce, like moussaka. The Ionian islands, interestingly, have a variety of pasta dishes, quite different from other Greek regions. This is inherited from the Venetians, who occupied the islands for a long period. Crete (the southernmost and also the largest of the Greek islands) has, on the other hand, great influence from Turkey and dishes here tend to be much more spiced than elsewhere in Greece, for example, *kheereeno kreeteeko*, a substantial pork chop dish baked and served with a variety of vegetables. When in Crete, visit the *zacharoplasteea*, selling snacks such as savoury spinach and cheese pies and sweet pastries. Another popular dish in this island is the *sofreeto* (a rich meat stew). Dried and preserved fruits are delicious, and fresh figs (*seeka*) as well as watermelon (*karpoozee*) are worth looking out for.

Greece can be a paradise for vegetarians, because among the many kinds of *mezedhes* and snacks there is a great variety of meatless food. A particularly good spread is a potato *mezedhes* in the Aegean (*leemneeoteekee salata*), leeks with sesame seeds (*prasa me seesamee*) or artichokes laced with lemon juice and olive oil (*angeenares a la poleeta*).

GREEK FOOD

Markets are worth visiting for their great array of tempting foods, well-displayed and reasonably priced. Vegetables, fruits (fresh and dried), nuts, at least two dozen different kinds of olives, as well as an abundance of meats and fish. Produce sold by small growers is very much in evidence and gives a comfortable old-fashioned feel to the place. Especially good food markets are the Athinás, in Athens, and the Odhós, in Crete. Athens has also many street food markets all over the city, each one opening at different days of the week. Apart from food, however, markets are also a good source of herbs of every kind, both for cooking and herbal teas, of which the Greeks are fond.

GREEK SPECIALITIES

One of Greece's national treasures is olive oil (*eleoladho*), used in great quantities by the Greeks and also exported. The splendid varieties of olives (*elyes*) from which it is made (themselves ubiquitous all over the country in their own right) are grown in a very favourable climate and terrain, and the percentage of extra-virgin oil is quite high. The best known eating olives are the very famous black *kalamata* olives, the Ionian green olives, the *nafpleeoo* (green and cracked), the black *throompes*, and the *amfeesas*, rounder and fleshier. However, taking into account all the other varieties, it is said that the country produces hundreds of different olives, both for olive oil, and for eating, preserved according to age-old traditions.

The *kalamata* olive oil is of course made from *kalamata* olives (which means a limited amount of this very special kind of oil). Most of the oil in Greece is produced mainly from the *regal* olive, which is a smaller variety of *kalamata* (known also as *koroneeko*). Even so, the number of olive oil varieties in Greece is vast. The oil is generally very well-flavoured and especially good to season the many kinds of salads served in Greece. Olives are Greece's oldest cultivated crop, dating back about four thousand years.

Although *feta* is probably the best known Greek cheese, *kefaloteeree*, *kaseree* and *gravyera*, a gruyère-style variety, are also very tasty. Try *meezeethra* made from goat's milk. When fresh, *feta* is white, crumbly and rather salty, and ideal for Greek salads.

Yoghurt is wonderful in Greece – thick, creamy and mild. It is used as a snack, or for breakfast, laced with honey, and for savoury dips. Yoghurts are either made with ewe's or cow's milk.

Breads include the popular pitta, olive flavoured rolls and small hard sticks studded with sesame seeds, or the ordinary bread that is truly delicious straight from the oven.

On the salad and dip front, *taramosalata*, is a very tasty kind of mousse of cod or mullet roe, thickened with potato or breadcrumbs and served for snacks and *mezedhes*. Other favourite dips are *tzatzeekee*, consisting of yoghurt, cucumber and garlic and *meleetzanosalata* a mousse based on aubergines. The best-known Greek salad is probably *khoreeateekee* which usually contains tomato, cucumber, olives, onions and feta cheese.

Cakes can be very sweet, such as *baklavas* (filo pastry with nuts, honey and syrup) and *lookoomadhes*, a sort of doughnut steeped in honey. Less sweet confections are walnut cake (*kareedhopeeta*) and a custard tart (*ghalaktobooreko*). Chocolate and marzipan are also good, as well as halva, a paste made with sesame seeds which is the base for many more dishes.

EATING OUT AND TYPES OF FOOD SERVED

There is a vast range of eating places all over Greece, many of them serving food all day, from light snacks to proper meals. As a rule, eating out is a relaxed and enjoyable activity and the Greek people themselves love to eat out. Even at stations and ferryboats one can find some interesting or at least filling snacks, such as *soovlakeea* (lamb or pork seasoned with herbs and barbecued). Street stalls have a variety of fast food, as well. Vegetarians can always bank on spinach pies (*spanakopeetes*) or lovely cheese ones (*teeropeetes*). For a sweet tooth the spicy and buttery cookies (*booteemata*) are ideal. Bakeries (*foornos*) have a splendid choice of light snacks. A good source of cheap and cheerful traditional food is obtainable at a *soovlatzeedeeko*,

GREEK FOOD

a modest establishment preparing a constant stream of bread with meat and vegetables on a skewer. Another popular, cheap place is an *oveleesteereeo*, specializing in kebab-style meat on pitta bread. If one wants to have *mezedhes* with wine, there are also specialist shops called *mezedhopoleeo*. More light snacks, sweets and cakes are available at a *zakharoplasteeo* (cake shop) or *ghalaktopoleeo* (dairy shop), serving also coffee and even alcoholic drinks, as well as yoghurt (*yaoortee*), icecream (*paghoto*), rice pudding (*reezoghalo*), custard tarts (*ghalaktobooreko*) and much more. All these places will be open most of the day, although some may close for the siesta. The *kafeneeo* (café), however, stays open from morning to late evening. It is a place much loved by Greeks – especially men – where there are various kinds of drinks available, mainly coffee itself (*kafes*), which can be sweet (*ghleeko*), medium sweet (*metreeo*) or without sugar (*sketo*). *Frappé* is a long, cold, coffee drink, very popular during the hot months and is made with instant coffee (*neskafe*). Tea, including herbal teas, and soft drinks are also served along with *ouzo* (of which there are many brands) and brandy (mainly Metaxa). Increasingly, there is also a range of snacks and salads at the *kafeneeo*, apart from the traditional fruits in syrup and other sweet delicacies. Some *oozeree* (ouzo shops), on the other hand, have a variety of savoury accompaniments to the drink, such as olives, cheese and nuts. Other *oozeree* actually offer an excellent menu of *mezedhes*.

Bars (*barakeea*), open all day and into the night, are the best places for beer (*beera*), normally ordered by the label name. Do not expect food here.

For proper, sit down meals, restaurants (*esteeatoreea*) and tavernas are the places to go. More select restaurants may need to be booked, and if there is anything in particular you would like to have, among their specialities, it may also be advisable to request beforehand that they keep some for you. Traditional restaurants and tavernas may invite you into their kitchens to see what is available and place your order accordingly. This way of choosing is especially popular for fish. You will see the fish displayed and can choose which one you want. Curiously, most of the food has been prepared already and will be served while it lasts (not necessarily hot from the oven!). At *esteeatoreea* hours generally revolve around 1 to 3pm for lunch, while dinner can be served from 6 to almost 11.30pm, in most places. Here you are likely to find traditional dishes like moussaka and other oven and casserole specialities. But there is always a good selection of *mezedhes*, salads and vegetables, as well. Normally, all dishes ordered will be brought to the table at the same time. If you prefer bottled wines, ask for the wine list (*kataloghos krasyon*), see page 71 for a selection of wines. As for desserts, variety is limited and sometimes confined to fruit in season (*freska froota*). Often Greeks finish their meals by going to one of the many excellent patisseries (*zakharoplasteeo*) for a sweet.

Certain restaurants take the additional name of *kultura* (culture) denoting that food and wine here are very refined, while *mayeereeo* is an establishment where food is at its simplest and cheapest, though good.

Tavernas are the most sought after eating places in Greece, be it on the mainland or the islands. Food in tavernas is down-to-earth, reasonable and healthy fare, and the more Greek customers they have the better the place will be.

Near the sea one will have all the great specialities prepared with fish and shellfish, i.e. small prawns (*ghareedhes*) or mussels (*meedheea*). *Mezedhes* are part of what tavernas have to offer and you can just feast on those, with a drink, at any time, without ordering main dishes. Some tavernas serve specialist food, such as those situated on the beach (*psarotaverna*), meaning fish taverna, with splendid seafood, or in the countryside serving barbecued meats, and often called *pseestareea* or *sta karvoona*. Game (*keeneeyee*) is also served at many tavernas and restaurants.

READING THE MENU

Starters or first courses are called *orekteeka*. The main course (*keereeo pyato*) can be fish or meat, or you might prefer to ask what the dish of the day is (*pyato tees eemeras*). However, the menu (*kataloghos*) in Greece is normally a list of *mezedhes*, followed by fish (*psareea*) and meat dishes (*kreas*), without actually referring to a first or second

DRINKS

course. Salads and vegetables are under the heading of *lachaneeka ke salateeka*. Whatever you order, it is generally served all at once. Desserts are found under *ghleeka* and include mainly fruit (*freska froota*).

ALCOHOLIC DRINKS

Greeks are not very heavy drinkers and most of the drinking is done outside the home, while socializing with friends or family. Whisky is a very popular drink in Greece. The Greeks also have a special liking for Cognac. Their traditional love for *ouzo* seems to be declining a little, but it is still popular, namely among tourists. There are various kinds of *ouzo*, according to region, but they all are similarly prepared, i.e. from the left-overs of pressed grapes, after their juice has been extracted for wine-making. The usual flavouring of this spirit is aniseed. *Ouzo* is quite strong on its own (over 45 per cent alcohol), so it is customary to take it as a refreshing long drink, mixed with water (*nero*) and ice, it then turns milky in appearance. It can be very pleasant and thirst-quenching on hot days. If you would like to have something to eat with it, you can, for example, order pistachio nuts (*feesteekeea eyeenees*), unless visiting an *oozeree*, where there is usually an excellent selection of *mezedhes*, perhaps less cheap than in other places, but worth trying.

Tseepooro is another famous spirit (a kind of eau-de-vie) and Crete also produces its own eau-de-vie called raki (*rakee*).

Metaxa (a local brandy-style spirit) is an obligatory drink after funerals, at least in larger cities, where cemeteries may have a coffee-shop where people can drink not only coffee but also Metaxa, accompanied by toasted dry bread. In the countryside relatives offer a meal of fish and wine to friends and family accompanying the funeral. Most of the Metaxa production (about 80 per cent) is exported.

A fair amount of beer (*beera*) is also drunk in Greece and there are now many pub-like establishments serving a good selection of beers. They are usually brewed in Greece under licence from foreign companies.

Wine (*krasee*) in Greece is mostly white. The main wine areas are the

Peloponnese, Macedonia and Attica, while sweet, dessert wines come from the north Aegean. One of the best-known white wines is *Retsina*, so-called because of its characteristic taste given by pine resin which is added to the wine during maturation. This practice was started many centuries ago as a means of preserving the wine, as well as giving it a special distinctive flavour. The best *Retsina* wine comes from the areas of Attica, Koropi and Markopoulo.

Boutari and *Kourtaki* wines are reasonably good and inexpensive. Better, dearer wines are, for example, *Strofilia* or *Semeli*. Many popular eating-places will serve cheap carafe wine from the barrel, generally produced locally and often rosé.

Here is a selection of Greek bottled wine:

Asprolithi dry white, modern type

Athanasiadhi dry white, modern type

Boutari Nemea red, from Rhodes (Ródos)

Boutari white, from Rhodes

Cambas white, from Rhodes

Domaine Carras whites and reds, from Macedonia

Gentilini white, from Crete

Chatzimihali a higher quality modern white wine

Himas wine from the barrel

Kourtakis retsina-type wine from Koropí and Markópoulo

Lazaridhi a higher quality modern white wine

Logado white from Crete

Mavrodaphne modern-type of sweet dessert wine, produced in Pátra

Tsantali Agioritiko higher quality white and red wines

Valerisio another expression for wine from the barrel, generally served in a carafe or jug

Other interesting wine labels are: *Merkouri*, *Semeli* and *Strofilia*.

DRINKS

OTHER DRINKS

beera beer

ghala milk

ghaz*oz*a fizzy soft drink (any kind)

kafes real, strong Greek coffee

    kafes frappe long, cool instant coffee drink (with or without milk)

    kafes me ghala milky coffee

    kafes metreeos medium-sweet black coffee

    kafes ghleekees very sweet black coffee

    kafes sketos unsweetened black coffee

leemonadha lemon drink

meelko chocolate drink with milk

metaleeko nero mineral water

metaxa brandy-type Greek spirit, more or less refined according to number of stars in the bottle

neskafe generic name given to instant coffee, no matter what brand

ouzo strong, white spirit extracted from left-over pressed grapes and flavoured with aniseed or staranise. Very popular. Taken as a long drink with wate (neró), it is a good summer drink. *Oúzo* is produced in many regions of Greece, wherever there is wine production.

portokaladha orange drink

rakee very strong white spirit prepared like oúzo but without flavourings. Produced in many parts of Greece and famous in Crete.

tsaee tea (not very popular in Greece)

tseepooro a firewater, popular in many Greek places

zestee sokolata hot chocolate

CYPRIOT FOOD

CYPRUS

Beautiful Cyprus, though a separate entity, has kept a very Greek atmosphere. The island has, however, other influences apart from that of Greece – Lebanon, Armenia, Syria, Italy, France, Britain and, of course, Turkey. This means that food has gradually absorbed different flavours which give Cypriot cuisine a subtle fusion and intriguing uniqueness.

The climate is kind to many crops and fruits, and everything is prepared with fresh, seasonal produce, from figs, to almonds and olive oil. But although Cyprus has olive oil, its use is more restrained than in Greece. Cracked wheat (*poorghooree*) is a common ingredient (used as a pilaf, with chicken) and one cannot get away from their delicious syrupy cakes and sweets. Kebabs in pitta bread are a favourite street food.

The structure of the meals follows quite closely that of Greece, with great emphasis on *mezedhes*, which will give an instant all embracing flavour of the island, with at least thirty different options to choose from. These delicacies are meant to be savoured slowly, for complete enjoyment. Start with green or black olives (*elyes*), followed perhaps by *takheenee* or *taramosalata* dips, eaten with the excellent local bread and *salata khoreeateekee*. Snails in tomato sauce (*saleengareea yakhnee*) are a local speciality, and so is octopus in red wine (*okhtapodhee krasato*). Fish is of course obligatory, perhaps *barboonee* (red mullet) or *kalamaree* (battered and fried squid rings). Grilled *khaloomee* cheese, *keftedhes* (meat balls), *loondza* (smoked pork) and *lookaneeka* (smoked local sausages) are other examples of special *mezedhes*. The meal may continue with moussaka or *steefadho* (braised meat). There are also kebabs, or grilled chicken and meat baked in a sealed oven (*klefteeko*). Afterwards fresh fruit will be in order, unless one could still fit in some fresh cheese and honey pastries (*boorekeea*).

Wholesome Cypriot dishes include good soups, such as *trapanos*, prepared with the popular cracked wheat and flavoured with yoghurt, or chicken broth with lemon and egg (*avgolemono*). There are also lovely vegetarian dishes, such as *loovya me lakhana*, made with black-eyed beans and various vegetables, laced with olive oil and lemon juice; *spanakopeeta*, spinach pie; *mookentra*, made with rice, onions and

CYPRIOT FOOD

lentils; or *meleetzanes yakhnee*, a casserole of tomatoes, aubergines and garlic.

Well-known meat dishes are *pasteetseeo*, a baked macaroni dish with a layer of meat, covered in bechamel sauce, or *tavas*, a highly seaoned meat casserole of beef or lamb with potatoes.

Desserts are very rich and irresistable, and part of the best Cypriot tradition. Try *kataeefee*, rolled up pastry in syrup; *ghalaktobooreko*, a custard tart; or *makhalepee*, a pudding in rosewater syrup. Other sweet Cypriot delicacies are *dhakteela* (almond cakes), *lookoomadhes* and the doughnut-like balls *peeseedes*, with syrup.

Markets are worth a lengthy visit to buy or just admire the fresh local produce bursting with colour and flavour, such as tomatoes, avocados, peppers, aubergines and herbs. Nectarines, plums, melons and grapes succeed each other throughout the summer months, while exquisite purple figs appear in late summer.

Fish and meat are excellent – goat being popular and very tasty. Pay also a visit to delicatessens, selling various kinds of local wild honey, olives of many sorts and cheeses (mainly *feta*, which is quite salty and soft, while *khaloomee* is a firmer cheese with a rubbery texture) made from ewe's, goat's and cow's milk. It can be served plain or grilled. Another good cheese is the ricotta-type *anaree*. A splendid dry cheese is called *kaskavalee*. Smoked pork meats, such as *loondza* (fillet), *kheeromeree* (leg), *lookaneeka* (spicy sausage), or *pastoorma* (very spicy sausage used to flavour barbecues) are well worth trying.

DRINKS

Strong coffee (*kafes*) is a great favourite in Cyprus. It is prepared in a special container with a long handle and boiled with sugar, in which case it can be medium-sweet (*metreeos*), or very sweet (*ghleekees*). Should you prefer it without sugar ask for *sketos*. If this sort of coffee is too strong order the instant: *neskafe*, or *nes*, for short.

Cyprus has long been producing good quality wines. The cultivation of grapes occupies a good percentage of the land, though only two kinds were traditionally produced: *Xynisteri*, for white wine, and *Mavro*, for red. In the last thirty or forty years, however, other varieties have been added, and this has resulted in a much wider choice of wines. made by expert winemakers. Despite this, the most famous wine is still an old, sweet wine, *Commandaria*, which according to tradition, started to be produced in a vast property in Kolossi, belonging to the Knights Hospitallars. This wine is made from raisins. It is always served at special occasions but, in ancient times, it was drunk in honour of the goddess Aphrodite, who according to legend, was born on Cyprus.

A popular local drink is sour brandy, consisting of brandy mixed with lemon juice.

MENU READER

αγγούρι *angooree* cucumber

αγκινάρες *angeenares* artichokes

αθερίνα *athereena* small fish, usually fried

αλάτι *alatee* salt

αρακάδες *arakadhes* peas

αρνάκι ψητό *arnakee pseeto* lamb chop grilled with herbs

αρνί *arnee* lamb

αρνί με βότανα *arnee me votana* lamb stewed with vegetables and
herbs

αρνίσιο *arneeseeo* lamb chops

αρνί ψητό *arnee pseeto* roast lamb

αστακός *astakos* lobster (often served with lemon juice and olive oil)

άσπρο *aspro* white (wine)

αυγά *avgha* eggs

αυγολέμονο *avgholemono* egg and lemon soup

αυγοτάραχο *avghotarakho* mullet roe (smoked)

αφελία *afeleea* pork in red wine with seasonings (Cyprus)

αχινοί *akheenee* sea urchin roes

αχλάδι *akhladhee* pear

αχλάδι στο φούρνο *akhladhee sto foorno* baked pear with syrup sauce

αχνιστό *akhneesto* steamed

βισινό κασέρι *veeseeno kaseree* kaséri cheese served with cherry
preserve

βοδινό *vodheeno* beef

γάλα *ghala* milk

γαλακτομπούρικο *ghalaktobooreko* custard tart

γαρίδες *ghareedhes* shrimps; prawns

γαρίδες γιουβέτσι *ghareedhes yoovetsee* prawns in tomato sauce
with feta

γεμιστά *yemeesta* stuffed vegetables

γιαούρτι *yaoortee* yoghurt

γιαούρτι με μέλι *yaoortee me melee* yoghurt with honey

γιαχνί *yakhnee* cooked in tomato sauce and olive oil

γίγαντες *yeeghantes* large butter beans

γκαζόζα *ghazoza* fizzy drink

γλυκά *ghlyka* dessert

γλυκά κουταλιού *ghlyka kootalyoo* dessert

γλώσσα *ghlosa* sole

γόπες *ghopes* bogue, a type of fish

γραβιέρα *ghravyera* cheese resembling gruyère

γύρος *yeeros* doner kebab

δάκτυλα *dhakteela* almond cakes

δαμάσκηνα *dhamaskeena* prunes with cream in wine sauce

δείπνο *dheepno* dinner

ελάχιστα ψημένο *elakheesta pseemeno* rare (meat)

ελιές *elyes* olives

ελιές τσακιστές *elyes tsakeestes* cracked green olives with coriander seeds and garlic (Cyprus)

ελιοτή *elyotee* olive bread

εστιατόριο *esteeatoreeo* restaurant

ζαχαροπλαστείο *zakharoplasteeo* cake shop

ζάχαρη *zakharee* sugar

ζελατίνα *zelateena* brawn

ζεστή σοκολάτα *zestee sokolata* hot chocolate

κάβουρας *kavooras* boiled crab

καλαμάκια *kalamrakya* small squid, fried

καλαμάρια *kalamareea* squid

καλαμάρια τηγανιτά *kalamareea teeghaneeta* fried squid

καλοψημένο *kalopseemeno* well done (meat)

κάπαρι *kaparee* pickled capers

καραβίδα *karaveedha* crayfish

καρότο *karoto* carrot

MENU READER

καρπούζι *karpoozee* watermelon

καρυδόπιτα *kareedhopeeta* walnut cake

κασέρι *kaseree* popular cheese made from sheep's milk, often served fried

καταΐφι *kataeefee* noodle-like small pastry drenched in syrup

κατάλογος *kataloghos* menu

κατάλογος κρασιών *kataloghos krasyon* wine list

κατσίκι *katseekee* roast kid

καφενείο *kafeneeo* café

καφές *kafes* coffee (Greek-style)

καφές γλυκύς *kafes ghleekees* very sweet coffee

καφές με γάλα *kafes me ghala* milky coffee

καφές μέτριος *kafes metreeos* medium-sweet coffee

καφές σκέτος *kafes sketos* coffee without sugar

κεράσια *keraseea* cherries

κεφαλότυρι *kefaloteeree* type of cheese, often served fried in olive oil

κεφτέδες *keftedhes* meat balls

κιδώνι *keedhonee* quince

κιδώνι στο φούρνο *keedhonee sto foorno* baked quince

κιμάς *keemas* mince

κλεφτικό *klefteeko* casserole with meat, potatoes and vegetables

κοκορέτσι *kokoretsee* skewed offal or liver, a special Easter dish

κολοκότες *kolokotes* pastries with pumpkins and raisins

κολοκυθάκια *kolokeethakeea* courgettes

κοτόπουλο *kotopoolo* chicken

κοτόπουλο ριγανάτο *kotopoolo reeghanato* grilled basted chicken with herbs

κουκκιά *kookya* broad beans

κουλούρια *koolooreea* bread rings

κουνέλλι *koonelee* rabbit

κουνουπίδι *koonoopeedhee* cauliflower

κουπέπια *koopepeea* stuffed vine leaves (Cyprus)

κουπές *koopes* meat pasties

κουραμπιέδες *koorambyedhes* small almond Xmas cakes

κρασί *krasee* wine

κρέας *kreas* meat

κρέμα *krema* creme

κρεμμύδια *kremeedheea* onions

κρητικη σαλάτα *salata kreeteekee* watercress salad

κυδώνια *keedhoneea* type of clams

κυνήγι *keeneeyee* game

κυρίο πιάτο *keereeo pyato* main course

λαβράκι *lavrakee* baked sea-bass

λαδερά *ladhera* vegetable casserole

λαχανά *lakhana* vegetables

λαχανικά *lakhaneeka* vegetables (menu heading)

λαχανό *lakhano* cabbage

λεμονάδα *lemonadha* lemon drink

λεμόνι *lemonee* lemon

λουκάνικα *lookaneeka* type of highly seasoned sausage

λουκουμάδες *lookoomadhes* small doughnut-type cake in syrup

λουκούμια *lookoomeea* shortbread served at weddings

λούντζα *loondza* loin of pork, marinated and smoked

μαγειρίτσα *mayecreetsa* soup made of lamb offal, special Easter dish

μανιτάρια *maneedareea* mushrooms

μαρίδες *mareedhes* small fish like sprats, served fried

μαριζόλες *mareezoles* meat cooked in olive oil and lemon juice

μαρούλι *maroolee* lettuce

μαύρο *mavro* red wine

μαυρομάτικα *mavromateeka* black-eyed peas

μεζές *mezes* mezedhes, selection of starters

μεζέδες *mezedhes* mezedhes, selection of starters

MENU READER

μεζεδοπωλείο *mezedhopoleeo* mezés shop

μέλι *melee* honey

μελιτζάνα *meleetzana* aubergine

μελιτζάνες ιμάμ *meleetzanes eemam* aubergines stuffed with tomato and onion

μελιτζανοσαλάτα *meleetzanosalata* aubergine mousse (dip)

μεσημεριανό *meseemereeano* lunch

μεταλλικό νερό *metaleeko nero* mineral water

μέτρια ψημένο *metreea pseemeno* medium (meat)

μήλα *meela* apples

μίλκο *meelko* milky chocolate drink

μοσχάρι *moskharee* veal

μουσακάς *moosakas* moussaka, layered aubergine, meat and potato, with white sauce

μπακλαβάς *baklavas* filo-pastry with nuts soaked in syrup

μπάμιες *bameeyes* okra (vegetable)

μπαρμπούνι *barboonee* red mullet

μπιφτέκια *beeftekya* rissole

μπουγάτσα *bougatsa* cheese cake or custard pastry sprinkled with sugar and cinnamon

μπουρέκι *boorekee* cheese potato and courgette pie

μπουρέκια *boorekeea* puff pastry filled with meat and cheese (Cyprus)

μπριάμ *breeam* ratatouille

μπριζόλα *breezola* steak (beef/pork)

μπριζόλα μοσχαρίσια *breezola moskhareeseea* veal chop

μύδια *meedheea* mussels

νερό *nero* water

ντολμάδες *dolmadhes* vine leaves, rolled up and stuffed with mince-meat and rice

ντομάτες *domates* tomatoes

ξιφίας *kseefeeas* swordfish

ξύδι *kseedhee* vinegar

οινοπωλείο *eenopoleeo* wine shop

ορεκτικά *orekteeka* first course/starter

οχταπόδια *okhtapodheea* octopus

οχταπόδι κρασάτο *okhtapodhee krasato* octopus in red wine sauce

παγωτό *paghoto* icecream

παϊδάκια *paeedhakeea* grilled lamb chops

παντζάρια *pandzareea* beetroot with seasonings

παξιμάδια *pakseemadheea* crispy bread (baked twice)

παπουτσάκια *papootsakeea* stuffed aubergines

παστίτσιο *pasteetseeo* baked pasta dish with a middle layer of meat

πατσάς *patsas* tripe soup

πατάτες *patates* potatoes

πατάτες τηγανιτές *patates teeghaneetes* chips

πεπόνι *peponee* melon

πέστροφα *pestrofa* trout

πιάτο της ημέρας *pyato tees eemeras* dish of the day

πιλάφι *peelafee* pilau rice

πιπέρι *peeperee* pepper

πιπεριές *peeperyes* peppers

πίττα *peeta* flat envelope of unleavened bread

πίττες *peetes* meaning pies, but they have different fillings, such as
meat, vegetables or cheese

πλακί *plakee* fish in tomato sauce

πορτοκαλάδα *portokaladha* orange drink

πορτοκάλια *portokalya* oranges

πουργούρι *poorghooree* cracked wheat (Cyprus)

πουργούρι πιλάφι *poorghooree peelafee* pilaf made of cracked wheat
(Cyprus)

πράσα με σησάμι *prasa me seesamee* leeks baked and sprinkled with
sesame seeds

MENU READER

πρωινό *proeeno* breakfast
ραβιόλι *raveeolee* pastry stuffed with cheese (Cyprus)
ραδίκια *radheekeea* chicory
ρεβίθια *reveetheea* chickpeas
ρίγανη *reeghanee* chicory
ροζέ *roze* rosé wine
ρύζι *reezee* rice
ρυζόγαλο *reezoghalo* rice pudding
σαγανάκι *saghanakee* mezedhes dish of fried cheese
σαλάτα *salata* salad
σαλατικά *salateeka* salads (menu heading)
σαλάχι *salakhee* ray
σαλιγκάρια *saleengareea* snails
σαλιγκάρια γιαχνί *saleengareea yakhnee* snails in tomato sauce
σαρδέλλες *sardhelles* sardines
σεφταλιά *seftalya* minced pork pasty
σικαλέσιο ψωμί *seekaleseeo psomee* rye bread
σικώτι *seekotee* liver
σκορδαλιά *skordhalya* garlic and walnut purée dip
σκορδαλιά με ψάρι τηγανιτό *skordhalya me psaree teeghaneeto* fried fish served with walnut and garlic sauce
σκόρδο *skordho* garlic
σουβλάκι *soovlakee* meat kebab
σούπα *soopa* soup
σουπιά *soopya* cuttlefish
σουτζουκάκια *sootzookakeea* highly seasoned meat balls
σοφρίτο *sofreeto* meat stew, highly seasoned (Corfu)
σπανάκι *spanakee* spinach
σπανακόπιτα *spanakopeeta* spinach pie
σπαράγγι *sparangee* asparagus
σπαράγγια και αγγινάρες *sparangeea ke angeenares* mezedhes of

    artichokes and asparagus in lemon juice

σπαράγγια σαλάτα *sparangeea salata* asparagus salad

σταφύλια *stafeeleea* grapes

στη σουβλά *stee soovla* spit-roasted

στιφάδο *steefadho* braised meat and tomato

στο φούρνο *sto foorno* baked in the oven

στρείδια *streedheea* oysters

σύκα *seeka* figs

σύκα στο φούρνο με μαυροδάφνη *seeka sto foorno me mavrodafnee* figs cooked in red wine sauce with spices

σχάρας *skharas* grilled

ταραμοσαλάτα *taramosalata* mousse of cod roe

ταχίνι *takheenee* sesame seed paste

τζατζίκι *tzatzeekee* cucumber and yoghurt dip

τόννος ψητός *tonos pseetos* grilled tuna with vegetables

τραπανός *trapanos* soup made of cracked wheat and yoghurt (Cyprus)

τσάι *tsaee* tea

τσιπούρα *tseepoora* type of sea bream

τσουρέκι *tsoorekee* festive bread

τυρί *teeree* cheese

τυροκαυτερή *teerokafteree* spicy dip made of cheese and peppers

τυρόπιτα *teeropeeta* cheese pie

τυροσαλάτα *teerosalata* starter made of cheese and herbs

φάβα *fava* yellow split peas or lentils, served in a purée with olive oil and capers

φαγγρί *fangree* sea bream

φακές *fakes* lentils

φασολάδα *fasoladha* very popular dish made with large white beans and herbs

φασολάκια *fasolakeea* green beans

φασόλια *fasoleea* haricot bean casserole

MENU READER

φέτα *feta* popular cheese, used in salads and other dishes
φλαούνες *flaoones* Easter cheese cake (Cyprus)
φράουλες *fraooles* strawberries
φρέσκα φρούτα *freska froota* fresh fruit
φρούτα *froota* fruit
φυστίκια *feesteekya* peanuts
φυστίκια Αιγίνης *feesteekya eyeenees* pistacchios
χαλβάς *khalvas* sesame seed sweet
χαλούμι *khaloomee* ewe's or goat's milk cheese, often grilled
χέλι καπνιστό *khelee kapneesto* smoked eel
χοιρινό *kheereeno* pork
χοιρινό κρηκικό *kheereeno kreeteeko* baked pork chops (Crete)
χοιρομέρι *kheeromeree* marinated, smoked ham
χόρτα *khorta* wild greens
χορτοφάγος *khortofaghos* vegetarian
χούμους *khoomoos* dip made with puréed chick peas
χταπόδι *khtapodhee* octopus, often grilled
χωριάτικη σαλάτα *choreeateekee salata* salad, Greek style with tomatoes, feta, cucumber and onions
ψάρι *psaree* fish
ψάρια καπνιστά *psareea kapneesta* smoked fish
ψάρια πλακί *psareea plakee* baked whole fish with vegetables and tomatoes
ψαρόσουπα *psarosoopa* seafood soup
ψαροταβέρνα *psarotaverna* fish taverna
ψησταρία *pseestareea* grill house
ψητό *pseeto* roast
ψωμάκι *psomakee* small bread
ψωμί *psomee* bread
ψωμι ολικής αλέσεως *psomee oleekees aleseos* wholemeal bread

DICTIONARY
english-greek
greek-english

a

a ένας / μία / ένα *enas* (masculine ο words) / *meea* (feminine η words) / *ena* (neuter το words)

abbey το μοναστήρι *to monasteeree*

abortion η άμβλωση *ee amvlosee*

about: *a book about Athens* ένα βιβλίο για την Αθήνα *ena veevleeo ya teen Atheena*
 at about ten o'clock περίπου στις δέκα *pereepoo stees dheka*

above πάνω από *pano apo*

abscess το απόστημα *to aposteema*

accident το ατύχημα *to ateekheema*

accommodation η στέγη *ee steyee*

ache ο πόνος *o ponos*

Acropolis η Ακρόπολη *ee Akropolee*

activities οι δραστηριότητες *ee dhrasteereeoteetes*

adaptor ο μετατροπέας *o metatropeas*

address η διεύθυνση *ee dheeeftheensee*
 what is your address? ποια είναι η διεύθυνσή σας; *pya eene ee dhee-eftheensee sas*

address book η ατζέντα *ee atzenda*

adhesive tape η συγκολλητική ταινία *ee seengoleeteekee teneea*

admission charge η είσοδος *ee eesodhos*

adult ο ενήλικος *o eneeleekos*

advance: *in advance* προκαταβολικώς *prokatavoleekos*

Aegean Sea το Αιγαίο (πέλαγος) *to eyeo (pelaghos)*

after μετά *meta*

afternoon το απόγευμα *to apoyevma*

aftershave το αφτερσέιβ *to aftershave*

afterwards αργότερα *arghotera*

again πάλι *palee*

ago: *a week ago* πριν μια βδομάδα *preen meea vdhomadha*

AIDS ΕΙΤΖ *e-eetz*

airbag ο αερόσακος *o aerosakos*

air conditioning ο κλιματισμός *o kleemateesmos*

air freshener το αποσμητικό χώρου *to aposmeeteeko khoroo*

airline η αεροπορική εταιρία *ee aeroporeekee etereea*

air mail αεροπορικώς *aeroporeekos*

air mattress το στρώμα για τη θάλασσα *to stroma ya tee thalasa*

airplane το αεροπλάνο *to aeroplano*

airport το αεροδρόμιο *to aerodhromeeo*

airport bus το λεωφορείο για το αεροδρόμειο *to leoforeeo ya to aerodhromeeo*

air ticket το αεροπορικό εισιτήριο *to aeroporeeko eeseeteereeo*

aisle *(in aircraft)* ο διάδρομος *o dheeadhromos*

alarm *(emergency)* ο συναγερμός *o seenayermos*

86

alarm clock το ξυπνητήρι *to kseepneeteeree*
alcohol το οινόπνευμα *to eenopnevma*
alcohol-free χωρίς οινόπνευμα *khorees eenopnevma*
alcoholic οινοπνευματώδης *eenopnevmatodhees*
all όλος *olos*
  all the milk όλο το γάλα *olo to ghala*
  all the time όλον τον καιρό *olon ton kero*
allergic to αλλεργικός σε *aleryeekos se*
alley το δρομάκι *to dhromakee*
allowance: *duty-free allowance* η επιτρεπόμενη ποσότητα *ee epeetrepomenee posoteeta*
all right *(agreed)* εντάξει *endaksee*
almond το αμύγδαλο *to ameeghdhalo*
also επίσης *epeesees*
always πάντα *panda*
am *see* **(to be) GRAMMAR**
ambulance το ασθενοφόρο *to asthenoforo*
America η Αμερική *ee amereekee*
American ο Αμερικανός / η Αμερικανίδα *o amereekanos / ee amereeka-needha*
amphitheatre το αμφιθέατρο *to amfeetheatro*
anaesthetic το αναισθητικό *to anestheeteeko*
anchor η άγκυρα *ee angeera*
anchovy η αντζούγια *ee andzooya*
and και *ke*
angina η στηθάγχη *ee steethangkhee*
angry θυμωμένος *theemomenos*
another άλλος *alos*
  another beer άλλη μία μπίρα *alee meea beera*
answer η απάντηση *ee apandeesee*
to answer απαντώ *apando*
answerphone ο αυτόματος τηλεφωνητής *o aftomatos teelefoneetees*
antacid το αντιοξινό *to andeeozeeno*
antibiotics τα αντιβιοτικά *ta andeeveeoteeka*
antihistamine το αντιισταμινικό *to andeestameeneeko*
antiques οι αντίκες *ee anteekes*
antiseptic το αντισηπτικό *to andeeseepteeko*
anywhere οπουδήποτε *opoodheepote*
apartment το διαμέρισμα *to dheeamereesma*
apartment block η πολυκατοικία *ee poleekateekeea*
aperitif το απεριτίφ *to apereeteef*
apple το μήλο *to meelo*
appendicitis η σκωληκοειδίτιδα *ee skoleekoeedheeteedha*
application form η αίτηση *ee eteesee*

appointment το ραντεβού *to randevoo*
apricot το βερίκοκο *to vereekoko*
archaeology η αρχαιολογία *ee arkheoloyeea*
architecture η αρχιτεκτονική *ee arkheetektoneekee*
are see **(to be)** GRAMMAR
arm το μπράτσο *to bratso*
armbands (for swimming) τα μπρατσάκια *ta bratsakya*
around γύρω *yeero*
to arrest συλλαμβάνω *seelamvano*
arrivals οι αφίξεις *ee afeeksees*
to arrive φτάνω *ftano*
art gallery η πινακοθήκη *ee peenakotheekee*
arthritis η αρθρίτιδα *ee arthreeteedha*
artichoke η αγκινάρα *ee angeenara*
ashtray το τασάκι *to tasakee*
asparagus το σπαράγγι *to sparangee*
aspirin η ασπιρίνη *ee aspeereenee*
  soluble aspirin διαλυόμενη ασπιρίνη *dheealeeomenee aspeereenee*
asthma το άσθμα *to asthma*
at σε (στο / στη / στο) *se (sto / stee / sto)*
atlas ο άτλαντας *o atlandas*

attractive (person) ελκυστικός *elkeesteekos*
aubergine η μελιτζάνα *ee meleetzana*
aunt η θεία *ee theea*
Australia η Αυστραλία *ee afstraleea*
Australian ο Αυστραλός / η Αυστραλίδα *o afstralos / ee afstraleedha*
automatic αυτόματος *aftomatos*
autoteller το ATM *to ey tee em*
autumn το φθινόπωρο *to ftheenoporo*
avalanche η χιονοστιβάδα *ee khyonosteevadha*
avocado το αβοκάντο *to avokado*
awful φοβερός *foveros*

B

baby το μωρό *to moro*
baby food οι βρεφικές τροφές *ee vrefeekes trofes*
baby milk το βρεφικό γάλα *to vrefeeko ghala*
baby's bottle το μπιμπερό *to beebero*
baby seat (in car) το παιδικό κάθισμα *to pedheeko katheesma*

baby-sitter η μπεϊμπισίτερ *ee babysitter*
baby wipes τα υγρά μαντηλάκια για μωρά *ta eeghra mandeelakya ya mora*
back (of a person) η πλάτη *ee platee*

backpack το σακκίδιο *to sakeedheeo*

bad *(of food)* χαλασμένος *khalasmenos*
(*of weather*) κακός *kakos*

bag *(small)* η τσάντα *ee tsanda*
(*suitcase*) η βαλίτσα *ee valeetsa*

baggage οι αποσκευές *ee aposkeves*

baggage reclaim η παραλαβή αποσκευών *ee paralavee aposkevon*

bait *(for fishing)* το δόλωμα *to dholoma*

baker's ο φούρνος *o foornos*

balcony το μπαλκόνι *to balkonee*

bald *(person, tyre)* φαλακρός *falakros*

ball η μπάλα *ee bala*

banana η μπανάνα *ee banana*

band *(musical)* η ορχήστρα *ee orkheestra*

bandage ο επίδεσμος *o epeedhesmos*

bank η τράπεζα *ee trapeza*

banknote το χαρτονόμισμα *to khartonomeesma*

bar το μπαρ *to bar*

barbecue η ψησταριά *ee pseestarya*

barber ο κουρέας *o kooreas*

barrel το βαρέλι *to varelee*

basil ο βασιλικός *o vaseeleekos*

basket το καλάθι *to kalathee*

basketball το μπάσκετ *to basket*

bath *(tub)* το μπάνιο *to banyo*
to take a bath κάνω μπάνιο *kano banyo*

bathing cap ο σκούφος του μπάνιου *o skoofos too banyoo*

bathroom το μπάνιο *to banyo*

battery η μπαταρία *ee batareea*

to be see **(to be) GRAMMAR**

beach η πλαζ *ee plaz* // η παραλία *ee paraleea*

bean *(haricot)* το φασόλι *to fasolee*
(*broad*) το κουκί *to kookee*
(*green*) το φασολάκι *to fasolakee*
(*soya*) η σόγια *ee soya*

beautiful όμορφος *omorfos*

bed το κρεββάτι *to krevatee*
double bed διπλό κρεββάτι *dheeplo krevatee*
single bed μονό κρεββάτι *mono krevatee*
twin beds δύο μονά κρεββάτια *dheeo mona krevatya*
sofa bed καναπές κρεββάτι *kanapes krevatee*

bedding τα κλινοσκεπάσματα *ta kleenoskepasmata*

bedroom η κρεββατοκάμαρα *ee krevatokamara*

beef το βοδινό *to vodheeno* // το μοσχάρι *to moskharee*

beer η μπίρα *ee beera*

b

beetroot το παντζάρι *to pandzaree*
before *(time)* πριν (από) *preen (apo)*
  (place) μπροστά από *brosta apo*
to begin αρχίζω *arkheezo*
behind πίσω από *peeso apo*
to believe πιστεύω *peestevo*
bell *(electric)* το κουδούνι *to koodhoonee*
below κάτω από *kato apo*
belt η ζώνη *ee zonee*
beside δίπλα *dheepla*
best ο καλύτερος *o kaleeteros*
better (than) καλύτερος (από) *kaleeteros (apo)*
between μεταξύ *metaksee*
bib η σαλιάρα *ee salyara*
bicycle το ποδήλατο *to podheelato*
big μεγάλος *meghalos*
bigger μεγαλύτερος *meghaleeteros*
bikini το μπικίνι *to beekeenee*
bill ο λογαριασμός *o logharyasmos*
bin το καλάθι των αχρήστων *to kalathee ton akhreeston*
bin liner η σακούλα σκουπιδιών *ee sakoola skoopeedhyon*

b

binoculars τα κιάλια *ta kyalya*
bird το πουλί *to poolee*
birth η γέννηση *ee yeneesee*
birth certificate το πιστοποιητικό γεννήσεως *to peestopyeetiko yeneeseos*
birthday τα γενέθλια *ta yenethleea*
  happy birthday! χρόνια πολλά *khronya pola*
biscuit το μπισκότο *to beeskoto*
bit: *a bit (of)* λίγο *leegho*
bite *(insect)* το τσίμπημα *to tseebeema*
bitten: *I have been bitten* με δάγκωσε *me dhangose*
bitter πικρός *peekros*
black μαύρος *mavros*
blackcurrant το μαύρο φραγκοστάφυλο *to mavro frangostafeelo*
blanket η κουβέρτα *ee kooverta*
bleach το λευκαντικό *to lefkandeeko*
to bleed αιμορραγώ *emoragho*
blister η φουσκάλα *ee fooskala*
blocked *(pipe)* βουλωμένος *voolomenos*
  (nose) κλειστή *kleestee*

b

blood group η ομάδα αίματος *ee omadha ematos*
blood pressure η πίεση αίματος *ee peeyesee ematos*
blouse η μπλούζα *ee blooza*

blow-dry στέγνωμα *steghnoma*

blue γαλάζιος *ghalazeeos*

boarding card το δελτίο επιβιβάσεως *to dhelteeo epeeveevaseos*

boarding house η πανσιόν *ee pansyon*

boat *(small)* η βάρκα *ee varka*
  (ship) το πλοίο *to pleeo*

boat trip η βαρκάδα *ee varkadha*

to boil βράζω *vrazo*

boiled βραστός *vrastos*
  boiled water βραστό νερό *vrasto nero*

bone το κόκκαλο *to kokalo*
  (fishbone) το ψαροκόκκαλλο *to psarokokalo*

book n το βιβλίο *to veevleeo*

to book *(room, tickets)* κλείνω *kleeno*

booking: to make a booking κλείνω θέση *kleeno thesee*

booking office *(railways, airlines, etc.)* το εκδοτήριο *to ekdhoteereeo*
  (theatre) το ταμείο *to tameeo*

bookshop το βιβλιοπωλείο *to veevleeopoleeo*

boots οι μπότες *ee botes*

border *(frontier)* τα σύνορα *ta seenora*

boring βαρετός *varetos*

boss ο / η προϊστάμενος *o / ee proeestamenos*

both και οι δυο *ke ee dheeo*

bottle το μπουκάλι *to bookalee*

bottle-opener το ανοιχτήρι *to aneekhteeree*

bowl το μπωλ *to bol*

box *(container)* το κιβώτιο *to keevotyo*
  (cardboard) το κουτί *to kootee*

box office το ταμείο *to tameeo*

boy το αγόρι *to aghoree*

boyfriend ο φίλος *o feelos*

bra το σουτιέν *to sootyen*

bracelet το βραχιόλι *to vrakheeolee*

to brake φρενάρω *frenaro*

brake fluid το υγρό των φρένων *to eeghro ton frenon*

brake light τα φώτα πεδήσεως *ta fota pedheeseos*

brakes τα φρένα *ta frena*

brandy το κονιάκ *to konyak*

bread το ψωμί *to psomee*
  (wholemeal) ψωμί ολικής αλέσεως *psomee oleekees aleseos*

to break σπάζω *spazo*

breakdown η βλάβη *ee vlavee*

breakdown van το συνεργείο διασώσεως *to seeneryeeo dheeasoseos*

breakfast το πρόγευμα *to proyevma*

b

breast το στήθος *to steethos*

to breathe αναπνέω *anapneo*

bride η νύφη *ee neefee*

bridegroom ο γαμπρός *o ghambros*

briefcase ο χαρτοφύλακας *o khartofeelakas*

to bring φέρνω *ferno*

Britain η Βρετανία *ee vretaneea*

British ο Βρετανός / η Βρετανίδα *o vretanos / ee vretaneedha*

brochure η μπροσούρα *ee brosoora*

broken σπασμένος *spasmenos*
   broken down χαλασμένος *khalasmenos*

bronze μπρούντζινος *broondzeenos*

brooch η καρφίτσα *ee karfeetsa*

brother ο αδελφός *o adhelfos*

brown καφέ *kafe*

bruise η μολώπη *ee molopee*

brush η βούρτσα *ee voortsa*

bucket ο κουβάς *o koovas*

buffet ο μπουφές *o boofes*

buffet car το βαγόνι εστιατόριο *to vaghonee esteeatoreeo*

bulb (light) ο γλόμπος *o ghlobos*

b

bumbag η μπανάνα *ee banana*

buoy η σημαδούρα *ee seemadhoora*

bureau de change (bank) ξένο συνάλλαγμα *kseno seenalaghma*

to burn καίω *keo*

burnt καμένος *kamenos*

to burst σκάζω *skazo*

bus το λεωφορείο *to leoforeeo*

business η δουλειά *ee dhoolya*

bus station ο σταθμός του λεωφορείου *o stathmos too leoforeeoo*

bus stop η στάση του λεωφορείου *ee stasee too leoforeeoo*

bus terminal το τέρμα του λεωφορείου *to terma too leoforeeoo*

bus tour η εκδρομή με λεωφορείο *ee ekdhromee me leoforeeo*

busy απασχολημένος *apaskholeemenos*

but αλλά *ala*

butcher's το κρεοπωλείο *to kreopoleeo*

butter το βούτυρο *to vooteero*

button το κουμπί *to koombee*

b

to buy αγοράζω *aghorazo*

by (beside) κοντά σε *konda se*
   (time) μέχρι *mekhree*

bypass η παρακάμψη *ee parakampsee*

C

cab το ταξί *to taksee*

cabbage το λάχανο *to lakhano*

cabin η καμπίνα *ee kabeena*

cable car το τελεφερίκ *to telefereek*

cable TV η δορυφορική τηλεώραση *ee dhoreeforeekee teeleorasee*

café το καφενείο *to kafeneeo*

cake το γλύκισμα *to ghleekeesma*

cake shop το ζαχαροπλαστείο *to zakharoplasteeo*

calculator ο υπολογιστής *o eepoloyeestees*

calendar το ημερολόγιο *to eemeroloyo*

to call φωνάζω *fonazo*

call n (telephone) η κλήση *ee kleesee*
  long-distance call η υπεραστική κλήση *ee eeperasteekee kleesee*

calm ήσυχος *eeseekhos*

camcorder η βιντεοκάμερα *ee veedeokamera*

camera η φωτογραφική μηχανή *ee fotoghrafeekee meekhanee*

to camp κατασκηνώνω *kataskeenono*

camping gas το γκαζάκι *to gazakee*

camping stove το πετρογκάζ *to petrogas*

campsite το κάμπινγκ *to camping*

to can vb : **I can** μπορώ *boro*
  you can μπορείς *borees*
  he can μπορεί *boree*
  we can μπορούμε *boroome*

can (of food) η κονσέρβα *ee konserva*
  (for oil) ο τενεκές *o tenekes*

Canada ο Καναδάς *o kanadhas*

Canadian ο Καναδός / η Καναδή *o Kanadhos/ee Kanadhee*

candle το κερί *to keree*

to cancel ακυρώνω *akeerono*

canoe το κανό *to kano*

can-opener το ανοιχτήρι *to aneekhteeree*

cappuccino το καπουτσίνο *to kapootseeno*

car το αυτοκίνητο *to aftokeeneeto*

car alarm ο συναγερμός *o seenayermos*

car ferry το φεριμπότ *to fereebot*

car keys τα κλειδιά αυτοκινήτου *ta kleedhya aftokeeneetoo*

car park το πάρκινγκ *to parking*

car radio το ραδιόφωνο αυτοκινήτου *to radhyofono aftokeeneetoo*

car seat (for children) το παιδικό κάθισμα αυτοκινήτου *to pedheeko katheesma aftokeeneetoo*

car wash το πλυντήριο αυτοκινήτων *to pleenteereeo aftokeeneeton*

C

carafe η καράφα *ee karafa*
caravan το τροχόσπιτο *to trokhospeeto*
card η κάρτα *ee karta*
cardigan η ζακέτα *ee zaketa*
careful προσεκτικός *prosekteekos*
carpet το χαλί *to khalee*
carriage *(railway)* το βαγόνι *to vaghonee*
carrot το καρότο *to karoto*
to carry κουβαλώ *koovalo*
case η υπόθεση *ee eepothesee*
  (suitcase) η βαλίτσα *ee valeetsa*
to cash *(cheque)* εξαργυρώνω *eksaryeerono*
cash τα μετρητά *ta metreeta*
cash desk το ταμείο *to tameeo*
cash dispenser το ATM *to ey tee em*
cashier ο ταμίας *o tameeas*
casino το καζίνο *to kazeeno*
cassette η κασέτα *ee kaseta*
castle το κάστρο *to kastro*
casualty department τα επείγοντα περιστατικά *ta epeeghonda pereesta-teeka*
cat η γάτα *ee ghata*
catalogue ο κατάλογος *o kataloghos*
to catch πιάνω *pyano*
  (bus, train, etc.) παίρνω *perno*
Catholic καθολικός *katholikos*
cauliflower το κουνουπίδι *to koonoopeedhee*
cave η σπηλιά *ee speelya*
CD το CD *to tse de*
celery το σέλινο *to seleeno*
cemetery το νεκροταφείο *to nekrotafeeo*
centimetre ο πόντος *o pondos*
central κεντρικός *kendreekos*
central locking *(car)* η αυτόματη κλειδαριά *ee aftomatee kleedharya*
centre το κέντρο *to kendro*
century ο αιώνας *o eonas*
certificate το πιστοποιητικό *to peestopyeeteeko*
chain η αλυσίδα *ee aleeseedha*
chair η καρέκλα *ee karekla*
champagne η σαμπάνια *ee sambanya*
change η αλλαγή *ee alayee*
  (money) τα ρέστα *ta resta*
to change αλλάζω *alazo*
changing room *(beach, sports)* το αποδυτήριο *to apodheeteereeo*

94

chapel το παρεκκλήσι *to parekleesee*

charcoal το ξυλοκάρβουνο *to kseelokarvoono*

charge η τιμή *ee teemee*

charter flight η ναυλωμένη πτήση *ee navlomenee pteesee*

cheap φτηνός *fteenos*

cheap rate *(for phone, etc)* η φτηνή ταρίφα *ee fteenee tareefa*

cheaper φτηνότερος *fteenoteros*

to check ελέγχω *elenkho*

check in περνώ από τον έλεγχο εισιτηρίων *perno apo ton elenkho eeseeteereeon*

check-in desk ο έλεγχος εισιτηρίων *o elenkhos eeseeteereeon*

cheek το μάγουλο *to maghoolo*

cheerio! γεια *ya*

cheers! *(your health)* στην υγειά σας *steen eeya sas*

cheese το τυρί *to teeree*

chemist's το φαρμακείο *to farmakeeo*

cheque η επιταγή *ee epeetayee*

cheque card η κάρτα επιταγών *ee karta epeetaghon*

cherry το κεράσι *to kerasee*

chestnut το κάστανο *to kastano*

chewing gum η τσίχλα *ee tseekhla*

chicken το κοτόπουλο *to kotopoolo*

chickenpox η ανεμοβλογιά *ee anemovloya*

chickpeas τα ρεβίθια *ta reveethcca*

child το παιδί *to pedhee*

children τα παιδιά *ta pedhya*

chilli το τσίλλι *to tseelee*

chilled: is the wine chilled? είναι κρύο το κρασί; *eene kreeo to krasee*

chips πατάτες τηγανητές *patates teeghaneetes*

chocolate η σοκολάτα *ee sokolata*

Christmas τα Χριστούγεννα *ta khreestooyena*
  merry Christmas! καλά Χριστούγεννα *kala khreestooyena*

church η εκκλησία *ee ekleeseea*

cigar το πούρο *to pooro*

cigarette το τσιγάρο *to tseegharo*

cigarette paper το τσιγαρόχαρτο *to tseegharokharto*

cinema ο κινηματογράφος *o keeneematoghrafos*

cistern το πηγάδι *to peeghadhee*

city η πόλη *ee polee*

clean καθαρός *katharos*

to clean καθαρίζω *kathareezo*

cleansing cream η κρέμα καθαρισμού *ee krema kathareesmoo*

client ο πελάτης / η πελάτισσα *o pelatees / ee pelateesa*

cliffs οι ύφαλοι *ee eefalee*

95

C

climbing η ορειβασία *ee oreevaseea*
climbing boots οι μπότες ορειβασίας *ee botes oreevaseeas*
clingfilm το σελαφάν *to selofan*
cloakroom η γκαρνταρόμπα *ee gardaroba*
clock το ρολόι *to roloee*
to close κλείνω *kleeno*
close adj (near) κοντινός *kondeenos*
  (weather) αποπνιχτικός *apopneekhteekos*
closed κλειστός *kleestos*
cloth το πανί *to panee*
  (for floor) το σφουγγαρόπανο *to sfoongaropano*
clothes τα ρούχα *ta rookha*
clothes line το σκοινί για τα ρούχα *to skeenee ya ta rookha*
clothes peg το μανταλάκι *to mandalakee*
cloudy συννεφιασμένος *seenefyasmenos*
cloves (spice) το γαρίφαλο *to ghareefalo*
club η λέσχη *ee leskhee*
coach (railway) το βαγόνι *to vaghonee*
  (bus) το πούλμαν *to poolman*
  (instructor) ο προπονητής *o proponeetees*
coach station ο σταθμός λεωφορείων *o stathmos leoforeeon*
coach trip το ταξίδι με πούλμαν *to takseedhee me poolman*

C

coast οι ακτές *ee aktes*
coastguard η ακτοφυλακή *ee aktofeelakee*
coat το παλτό *to palto*
coat hanger η κρεμάστρα *ee kremastra*
cockroach η κατσαρίδα *ee katsareedha*
cocoa το κακάο *to kakao*
coffee ο καφές *o kafes*
  black coffee σκέτος καφές *sketos kafes*
  white coffee καφές με γάλα *kafes me ghala*
coin το νόμισμα *to nomeesma*
colander το σουρωτήρι *to sooroteeree*
cold κρύος *kreeos*
  I have a cold είμαι κρυωμένος *eeme kreeomenos*
  I'm cold κρυώνω *kreeono*
cold sore ο έρπητας *o erpeetas*
colour το χρώμα *to khroma*
colour blind δαλτωνικός *dhaltoneekos*
colour film το έγχρωμο φιλμ *to enkhromo feelm*
comb η χτένα *ee khtena*

C

to come έρχομαι *erkhome*
to come back γυρίζω *yeereezo*
to come in μπαίνω *beno*
comfortable αναπαυτικός *anapafteekos*

communion *(holy)* η θεία κοινωνία *ee theea keenoneea*
company *(firm)* η εταιρία *ee etereea*
compartment το διαμέρισμα *to dheeamereesma*
compass ο μπούσουλας *o boosoolas*
to complain παραπονούμαι *paraponoome*
compulsory υποχρεωτικός *eepokhreoteekos*
computer ο κομπιούτερ *o computer*
computer software το software *to software*
concert η συναυλία *ee seenavleea*
concert hall το μέγαρο μουσικής *to megharo mooseekees*
condition η κατάσταση *ee katastasee*
condom το προφυλακτικό *to profeelakteeko*
conductor *(bus)* ο εισπράκτορας *o eespraktoras*
  (train) ο ελεγκτής *o elenktees*
conference η διάσκεψη *ee dheeaskepsee*
to confirm επιβεβαιώνω *epeeveveono*
congratulations! συγχαρητήρια *seenkhareeteereea*
connection *(trains, etc.)* η σύνδεση *ee seendhesee*
to be constipated έχω δυσκοιλιότητα *ekho dheeskeeleeoteeta*
consulate το προξενείο *to prokseneeo*
to contact επικοινωνώ *epeekeenono*
contact lenses οι φακοί επαφής *ee fakee epafees*
contact lens cleaner το καθαριστικό διάλυμα *to kathareesteeko dheealeema*
contraceptives τα αντισυλληπτικά *ta andeeseeleepteeka*
contract το συμβόλαιο *to seemvoleo*
to cook μαγειρεύω *mayeerevo*
cooker η κουζίνα *ee koozeena*
cool δροσερός *dhroseros*
cool box *(for picnics)* το ψυγειάκι *to pseeyeeakee*
copper ο χάλκος *o khalkos*
to copy *(photocopy)* φωτοτυπώ *fototeepo*
copy *n* το αντίγραφο *to andeeghrafo*
coral το κοράλλι *to koralee*
coriander ο κόλιαντρος *o kolyantros*
corkscrew το τιρμπουσόν *to teerbooson*
corn *(sweet corn)* το καλαμπόκι *to kalambokee*
corner η γωνία *ee ghoneea*
cornflakes τα κορνφλέικς *ta cornflakes*
cortisone η κορτιζόνη *ee korteezonee*
cosmetics τα καλλυντικά *ta kaleendeeka*
to cost στοιχίζω *steekheezo*
cotton το βαμβάκι *to vamvakee*

C

cotton buds οι μπατουέτες *ee batooetes*
cotton wool το βαμβάκι *to vamvakee*
couchette η κουκέτα *ee kooketa*
cough ο βήχας *o veekhas*
country η χώρα *ee khora*
  (not town) η εξοχή *ee eksokhee*
couple *(two people)* το ζευγάρι *to zevgharee*
courgette το κολοκυθάκι *to kolokeethakee*
courier *(for tourists)* ο / η συνοδός *o / ee seenodhos*
course *(meal)* το πιάτο *to pyato*
cousin ο εξάδελφος / η εξαδέλφη *o eksadhelfos / ee eksadhelfee*
cover charge το κουβέρ *to koover*
crab το καβούρι *to kavooree*
cramp η κράμπα *o krampa*
to crash συγκρούομαι *seengkrooome*
crash η σύγκρουση *ee seengroosee*
crash helmet το κράνος *to kranos*
cream η κρέμα *ee krema*
credit card η πιστωτική κάρτα *ee peestoteekee karta*
crime το έγκλημα *to engkleema*
crisps τα πατατάκια *ta patatakya*
croquette η κροκέτα *ee kroketa*

C

cross ο σταυρός *o stavros*
to cross διασχίζω *dheeaskheezo*
crossroads το σταυροδρόμι *to stavrodhromee*
crowded γεμάτος *yematos*
cruise η κρουαζιέρα *ee krooazyera*
crutches τα δεκανίκια *ta dhekaneekya*
cucumber το αγγούρι *to angooree*
cup το φλυτζάνι *to fleedzanee*
cupboard το ντουλάπι *to doolapee*
currant η σταφίδα *ee stafeedha*
current *(electric)* το ρεύμα *to revma*
cushion το μαξιλάρι *to makseelaree*
custard η κρέμα *ee krema*
customer ο πελάτης *o pelatees*
customs το τελωνείο *to teloneeo*
to cut κόβω *kovo*
cut το κόψιμο *to kopseemo*

C

cutlery τα μαχαιροπήρουνα *ta makheropeeroona*
to cycle ποδηλατώ *podheelato*
cyst η κύστις *ee keestees*
cystitis η κυστίτιδα *ee keesteeteedha*

D

daily ημερήσιος *eemereeseeos*

dairy products τα γαλακτοκομικά προϊόντα *ta ghalaktokomeeka proeeonda*

damage η ζημιά *ee zeemya*

damp υγρός *eeghros*

dance *n* ο χορός *o khoros*

to dance χορεύω *khorevo*

danger ο κίνδυνος *o keendheenos*

dangerous επικίνδυνος *epeekeendheenos*

dark *(colour)* σκούρο *skooro*
 it's dark είναι σκοτεινά *eene skoteena*

date η ημερομηνία *ee eemeromeeneea*
 what's the date? τι ημερομηνία είναι; *tee eemeromeeneea eene*

date of birth η ημερομηνία γεννήσεως *ee eemeromeeneea yeneeseos*

daughter η κόρη *ee koree*

day η μέρα *ee mera*

dead νεκρός *nekros*

dear αγαπητός *aghapeetos*
 (expensive) ακριβός *akreevos*

decaffeinated χωρίς καφεΐνη *khorees kafeeenee*

deck chair η ξαπλώστρα *ee ksaplostra*

to declare δηλώνω *dheelono*

deep βαθύς *vathees*

deep freeze η κατάψυξη *ee katapseeksee*

to defrost ξεπαγώνω *ksepaghono*

delay η καθυστέρηση *ee katheestereesee*

delayed καθυστερισμένος *katheestereesmenos*

delicious νόστιμος *nosteemos*

dentist ο / η οδοντογιατρός *o / ee odhondoyatros*

dentures η οδοντοστοιχία *ee odhondosteekheea*

deodorant το αποσμητικό *to aposmeeteeko*

department store το πολυκατάστημα *to poleekatasteema*

departure η αναχώρηση *ee anakhoreesee*

departure lounge η αίθουσα αναχωρήσεων *ee ethoosa anakhoreeseon*

deposit *(part payment)* η προκαταβολή *ee prokatavolee*

dessert το επιδόρπιο *to epeedhorpeeo*

details οι λεπτομέρειες *ee leptomereeyes*

detergent το απορρυπαντικό *to aporeepandeeko*

detour: to make a detour βγαίνω από το δρόμο *vyeno apo to dhromo*

to develop αναπτύσσω *anapteeso*

diabetic διαβητικός *dheeaveeteekos*

to dial παίρνω αριθμό *perno areethmo*

dialling code ο τηλεφωνικός κώδικας *o teelefoneekos kodheekas*

d

diamond το διαμάντι to dheeamandee
diapers οι πάνες ee panes
diarrhoea η διάρροια ee dheeareea
diary το ημερολόγιο to eemeroloyo
dictionary το λεξικό to lekseeko
diesel το ντίζελ to deezel
diet η δίαιτα ee dheeeta
   I'm on a diet κάνω δίαιτα kano dheeeta
different διαφορετικός dheeaforeteekos
difficult δύσκολος dheeskolos
dinghy η μικρή βάρκα ee meekree varka
dining room η τραπεζαρία ee trapezareea
dinner το δείπνο to dheepno
direct άμεσος amesos
directory *(telephone)* ο τηλεφωνικός κατάλογος o teelefoneekos kataloghos
directory enquiries οι πληροφορίες καταλόγου ee pleeroforeeyes kataloghoo
dirty ακάθαρτος akathartos
disabled ανάπηρος anapeeros
disco η ντισκοτέκ ee deeskotek
discount η έκπτωση ee ekptosee

d

dish το πιάτο to pyato
dish towel η πετσέτα πιάτων ee petseta pyaton
dishwasher το πλυντήριο πιάτων to pleenteereeo pyaton
disinfectant το απολυμαντικό to apoleemandeeko
disk *(floppy)* η δισκέτα ee dheesketa
distilled water το απεσταγμένο νερό to apestaghmeno nero
divorced ο χωρισμένος / η χωρισμένη o khoreesmenos / ee khoreesmenee
dizzy ζαλισμένος zaleesmenos
to do: *I do* κάνω kano
   you do κάνεις kanees
doctor ο / η γιατρός o / ee yatros
documents τα έγγραφα ta engrafa
dog το σκυλί to skeelee
doll η κούκλα ee kookla
dollar το δολάριο to dholareeo
door η πόρτα ee porta
donkey το γαϊδούρι to ghaeedhooree
donor card η κάρτα δότη ee karta dhotee

d

double διπλός dheeplos
double bed το διπλό κρεββάτι to dheeplo krevatee
double room το δίκλινο δωμάτιο to dheekleeno dhomateeo
down: *to go down* κατεβαίνω kateveno

downstairs κάτω *kato*
drachmas δραχμές *dhrakhmes*
drain η αποχέτευση *ee apokhetefsee*
draught *(of air)* το ρεύμα *to revma*
draught lager η μπίρα από βαρέλι *ee beera apo varelee*
drawer το συρτάρι *to seertaree*
drawing το σχέδιο *to skhedheeo*
dress το φόρεμα *to forema*
to dress ντύνομαι *deenome*
dressing *(for salad)* το λαδολέμονο *to ladholemono*
dressing gown η ρόμπα *ee roba*
drill τρυπώ *treepo*
drink *n* το ποτό *to poto*
  to have a drink παίρνω ένα ποτό *perno ena poto*
to drink πίνω *peeno*
drinking water το πόσιμο νερό *to poseemo nero*
to drive οδηγώ *odheegho*
driver ο οδηγός *o odheeghos*
driving licence η άδεια οδήγησης *ee adheea odheeyeesees*
to drown πνίγομαι *pneeghome*
drug *(illegal)* το ναρκωτικό *to narkoteeko*
  (medicine) το φάρμακο *to farmako*
drunk μεθυσμένος *metheesmenos*
dry *n* στεγνός *steghnos*
to dry στεγνώνω *steghnono*
dry-cleaners το καθαριστήριο *to kathareesteereeo*
duck η πάπια *ee papya*
due: when is the train due? πότε θα φτάσει το τραίνο; *pote tha ftasee to treno*
dummy η πιπίλα *ee peepeela*
during κατά τη διάρκεια *kata tee dheearkeea*
dust η σκόνη *ee skonee*
duvet το πάπλωμα *to paploma*
duvet cover η παπλωματοθήκη *ee paplomatotheekee*

E

each κάθε *kathe*
  100 drachmas each εκατό δραχμές ο καθένας *ekato drakhmes o kathenas*
ear το αυτί *to aftee*
earache: I have earache με πονάει το αυτί μου *me ponaee to aftee moo*
earlier νωρίτερα *noreetera*
early νωρίς *norees*
earrings τα σκουλαρίκια *ta skoolareekya*
earthquake ο σεισμός *o seesmos*

east η ανατολή *ee anatolee*

Easter το Πάσχα *to paskha*

easy εύκολος *efkolos*

to eat τρώω *tro-o*

eel το χέλι *to khelee*

egg το αβγό *to avgho*
   fried eggs αβγά τηγανητά *avgha teeghaneeta*
   boiled eggs αβγά βραστά *avgha vrasta*
   poached eggs αβγά ποσέ *avgha pose*

either ... or ή ... ή *ee ...ee // είτε ... είτε *eete ... eete*

elastic το ελαστικό *to elasteeko*

elastic band το λαστιχάκι *to lasteekhakee*

electrician ο ηλεκτρολόγος *o eelektrologhos*

electricity meter ο μετρητής ηλεκτρισμού *o metreetees eelektreesmoo*

electric razor η ξυριστική μηχανή *ee kseereesteekee meekhanee*

e-mail το e-mail *to e-mail*

e-mail address η e-mail διεύθυνση *ee e-mail dheeeftheensee*

embassy η πρεσβεία *ee presveea*

emergency: *its an emergency* είναι επείγον περιστατικό *eene epeeghon pereestateeko*

empty άδειος *adheeos*

end το τέλος *to telos*

engaged *(to marry)* αρραβωνιασμένος / η *aravonyasmenos/ee*
   (toilet) κατειλημμένη *kateeleemenee*
   (phone) μιλάει *meelaee*

engine η μηχανή *ee meekhanee*

England η Αγγλία *ee angleea*

English ο Άγγλος / η Αγγλίδα *o anglos / ee angleedha*

to enjoy oneself διασκεδάζω *dheeaskedhazo*

enough αρκετά *arketa*
   enough bread αρκετό ψωμί *arketo psomee*

enquiry desk / office το γραφείο πληροφοριών *to ghrafeeo pleeroforeeon*

to enter μπαίνω *beno*

entertainment η ψυχαγωγία *ee pseekhaghoyeea*

entrance η είσοδος *ee eesodhos*

entrance fee η τιμή εισόδου *ee teemee eesodhoo*

envelope ο φάκελος *o fakelos*

equipment ο εξοπλισμός *o eksopleesmos*

escalator η κυλιόμενη σκάλα *ee keelyomenee skala*

especially ειδικά *eedheeka*

essential απαραίτητος *apareeteetos*

Eurocheque η ευρωεπιταγή *ee evroepeetayee*

Europe η Ευρώπη *ee evropee*

even number ο ζυγός αριθμός *o zeeghos areethmos*

evening το βράδυ *to vradhee*
  this evening απόψε *apopse*
  in the evening το βράδυ *to vradhee*
every κάθε *kathe*
everyone όλοι *olee*
everything όλα *ola*
exact ακριβής *akreevees*
examination η εξέταση *ee eksetasee*
excellent εξαιρετικός *eksereteekos*
except εκτός από *ektos apo*
excess luggage επί πλέον αποσκευές *epee pleon aposkeves*
exchange rate η τιμή του συναλλάγματος *ee teemee too seenalaghmatos*
excursion η εκδρομή *ee ekdhromee*
excuse me με συγχωρείτε *me seenkhoreete*
exhaust pipe η εξάτμιση *ee eksatmeesee*
exhibition η έκθεση *ee ekthese*
exit η έξοδος *ee eksodhos*
expensive ακριβός *akreevos*
expert ο / η ειδικός *o / ee eedheekos*
to expire λήγω *leegho*
expired έχει λήξει *ekhee leeksee*
to explain εξηγώ *ekseegho*
express *(train)* η ταχεία *ee takheea*
express letter το κατεπείγον γράμμα *to katepeeghon ghrama*
extra: it costs extra στοιχίζει επιπλέον *steekheezee epeepleon*
  extra money περισσότερα χρήματα *pereesotera khreemata*
eyes τα μάτια *ta matya*

F

fabric το ύφασμα *to eefasma*
face το πρόσωπο *to prosopo*
facilities οι ευκολίες *ee efkoleeyes*
factory το εργοστάσιο *to erghostaseeo*
to faint λιποθυμώ *leepotheemo*
fainted λιποθύμησε *leepotheemeese*
fair *adj (hair)* ξανθός *ksanthos*
fair *n (commercial)* η έκθεση *ee ekthese*
  (fun fair) το λουνα-πάρκ *to loonapark*
to fall πέφτω *pefto*
  he / she has fallen έπεσε *epese*
family η οικογένεια *ee eekoyenya*
famous διάσημος *dheeaseemos*
fan *(electric)* ο ανεμιστήρας *o anemeesteeras*
fan belt το λουρί του ψυγείου *to looree too pseeyeeoo*

103

f

far μακριά *makreea*

fare *(bus, train)* το εισιτήριο *to eeseeteereeo*

farm το αγρόκτημα *to aghrokteema*

fast γρήγορα *ghreeghora*

fat *adj* χοντρός *khondros*

fat *n* το λίπος *to leepos*

father ο πατέρας *o pateras*

father-in-law ο πεθερός *o petheros*

fault *(mistake)* το λάθος *to lathos*
  it is not my fault δε φταίω εγώ *dhe fteo egho*

favourite ο πιο αγαπημένος *o pyo aghapeemenos*

fax το φαξ *fax*

feather *(of bird)* το φτερό *to ftero*

to feed τρέφω *trefo*
  (baby) ταΐζω *taeezo*

to feel αισθάνομαι *esthanome*
  I feel sick θέλω να κάνω εμετό *thelo na kano emeto*

female θηλυκός *theeleekos*

ferry το φεριμπότ *to fereebot*

festival το φεστιβάλ *to festeeval*

to fetch φέρνω *ferno*

f

fever ο πυρετός *o peeretos*

few: a few μερικοί / μερικές / μερικά *mereekee (masculine) / mereekes (feminine) / mereeka (neuter)*

fiancé(e) ο αρραβωνιαστικός / η αρραβωνιαστικιά *o aravonyasteekos / ee aravonyasteekya*

field το χωράφι *to khorafee*

file *(nail)* η λίμα *ee leema*
  (computer) το αρχείο *to arkheeo*

to fill γεμίζω *yemeezo*
  fill it up! *(car)* γεμίστε το *yemeeste to*

fillet το φιλέτο *to feeleto*

filling *(in cake, etc.)* η γέμιση *ee yemeesee*
  (in tooth) το σφράγισμα *to sfrayeesma*

film *(for camera)* το φιλμ *to feelm*
  (in cinema) η ταινία *ee teneea*

filter το φίλτρο *to feeltro*

to finish τελειώνω *teleeono*

fire *(heater)* η θερμάστρα *ee thermastra*
  fire! φωτιά! *fotya!*
  fire brigade η πυροσβεστική *ee peerosvesteekee*
  fire extinguisher ο πυροσβεστήρας *o peerosvesteeras*

fireworks τα πυροτεχνήματα *ta peerotekhneemata*

first πρώτος *protos*

first aid οι πρώτες βοήθειες *ee protes voeetheeyes*

first class *(seat, etc.)* η πρώτη θέση *ee protee thesee*
first floor ο πρώτος όροφος *o protos orofos*
first name το όνομα *to onoma*
fish το ψάρι *to psaree*
to fish ψαρεύω *psarevo*
fishing rod το καλάμι ψαρέματος *to kalamee psarematos*
fit *(healthy)* υγιής *eeyee-ees*
to fix επιδιορθώνω *epeedheeorthono*
　(arrange) κανονίζω *kanoneezo*
fizzy *(drink)* αεριούχο *aeryookho*
flash *(on camera)* το φλας *to flas*
flask το θερμός *to thermos*
flat *(apartment)* το διαμέρισμα *to dheeamereesma*
flat tyre: I have a flat tyre έχω σκασμένο λάστιχο *ekho skasmeno lastcokho*
flea ο ψύλλος *o pseelos*
flight η πτήση *ee pteesee*
flippers *(swimming)* τα βατραχοπέδιλα *ta vatrakhopedheela*
flood η πλημμύρα *ee pleemeera*
floor το πάτωμα *to patoma*
　(storey) ο όροφος *o orofos*
flour το αλεύρι *to alevree*
flower το λουλούδι *to looloodhee*
flu η γρίπη *ee ghreepee*
to fly πετώ *peto*
fly η μύγα *ee meegha*
to follow ακολουθώ *akolootho*
food το φαγητό *to fayeeto*
food poisoning η τροφική δηλητηρίαση *ee trofeekee dheeleeteereeasee*
foot το πόδι *to podhee*
football το ποδόσφαιρο *to podhosfero*
for για *ya*
foreign ξένος *ksenos*
forest το δάσος *to dhasos*
to forget ξεχνώ *ksekhno*
fork το πηρούνι *to peeroonee*
　(in road) η διακλάδωση *ee dheeakladhosee*
fortnight το δεκαπενθήμερο *to dhekapentheemero*
fountain το σιντριβάνι *to seendreevanee*
fracture *(of bone)* το κάταγμα *to kataghma*
France η Γαλλία *ee ghaleea*
free ελεύθερος *eleftheros*
　(costing nothing) δωρεάν *dhorean*
to freeze *(food)* ψύχω *pseekho*

f

freezer ο καταψύκτης *o katapseektees*
French *(thing)* γαλλικός *ghaleekos*
French beans τα φασολάκια *ta fasolakya*
frequent συχνός *seekhnos*
fresh φρέσκος *freskos*
fridge το ψυγείο *to pseeyeeo*
fried τηγανητός *teeghaneetos*
friend ο φίλος / η φίλη *o feelos / ee feelee*
from από *apo*
front *(part)* το μπροστινό (μέρος) *to brosteeno (meros)*
  in front μπροστά *brosta*
frozen *(water)* παγωμένος *paghomenos*
  (food) κατεψυγμένος *katepseeghmenos*
fruit τα φρούτα *ta froota*
fruit juice ο χυμός φρούτων *o kheemos frooton*
fruit salad η φρουτοσαλάτα *ee frootosalata*
frying pan το τηγάνι *to teeghanee*
fuel τα καύσιμα *ta kafseema*
fuel pump η αντλία καυσίμων *ee andleea kafseemon*
full γεμάτος *yematos*
full board (η) πλήρης διατροφή *(ee) pleerees dheeatrofee*

f

fumes *(of car)* τα καυσαέρια *ta kafsaereea*
funeral η κηδεία *ee keedheea*
funny αστείος *asteeos*
fur η γούνα *ee ghoona*
furniture τα έπιπλα *ta epeepla*
fuse η ασφάλεια *ee asfaleea*
fuse box ο ηλεκτρικός πίνακας *o eelektreekos peenakas*

G

gallery *(art)* η πινακοθήκη *ee peenakotheekee*
game το παιχνίδι *to peghneedhee*
  (to eat) το κυνήγι *to keeneeyee*
garage *(for parking car)* το γκαράζ *to garaz*
garden ο κήπος *o keepos*
garlic το σκόρδο *to skordho*
gas το γκάζι *to gazee*
gas cooker η γκαζιέρα *ee ghaszyera*
gas cylinder η φιάλη γκαζιού *ee feealee gazyoo*
gate *(at airport)* η έξοδος *ee eksodhos*

g

gears οι ταχύτητες *ee takheeteetes*
  first gear πρώτη *protee*
  second gear δεύτερη *dhefteree*
  third gear τρίτη *treetee*

106

fourth gear τετάρτη *tetartee*
neutral νεκρή *nekree*
reverse όπισθεν *opeesthen*

gearbox το κιβώτιο ταχυτήτων *to keevotyo takheeteeton*

gents (toilet) Ανδρών *andhron*

genuine γνήσιος *ghneeseeos*

germs τα μικρόβια *ta meekroveea*

German measles η ερυθρά *ee ereethra*

to get παίρνω *perno*
(fetch) φέρνω *ferno*

to get in (car, etc.) μπαίνω *beno*

to get off (from bus) κατεβαίνω από *kateveno apo*

to get on (bus) ανεβαίνω στο λεωφορείο *aneveno sto leoforeeo*

to get through (on the phone) συνδέομαι *seendheome*

gift το δώρο *to dhoro*

gift shop το κατάστημα δώρον *to katasteema dhoron*

gin το τζιν *to gin*

ginger η πιπερόρριζα *ee peeperoreeza*

girl το κορίτσι *to koreetsee*

girlfriend η φίλη *ee feelee*

to give δίνω *dheeno*

to give back επιστρέφω *epeestrefo*

glass (to drink from) το ποτήρι *to poteeree*
a glass of water ένα ποτήρι νερό *ena poteeree nero*

glasses (spectacles) τα γυαλιά *ta yalya*

gloves τα γάντια *ta ghandeea*

glucose η γλυκόζη *ee ghleekozee*

glue n η κόλλα *ee kola*

to glue κολλώ *kolo*

to go πηγαίνω *peeyeno*
I go / I am going πηγαίνω *peeyeno*
you go / you are going πηγαίνεις *peeyenees*
we go / we are going πηγαίνουμε *peeyenoome*

to go back γυρίζω πίσω *yeereezo peeso*

to go down κατεβαίνω *kateveno*

to go in μπαίνω *beno*

to go out βγαίνω *vyeno*

to go up ανεβαίνω *aneveno*

goat η κατσίκα *ee katseeka*

goggles τα γυαλιά *ta yalya*

gold ο χρυσός *o khreesos*
(made of gold) χρυσός *khreesos*

golf το γκολφ *to golf*

golf course το γήπεδο του γκολφ *to yeepedho too golf*

good καλός *kalos*

g

g

g

g

good afternoon χαίρετε *kherete*
goodbye αντίο *adeeo*
good day καλημέρα *kaleemera*
good evening καλησπέρα *kaleespera*
good morning καλημέρα *kaleemera*
good night καληνύχτα *kaleeneekhta*
goose η χήνα *ee kheena*
gram το γραμμάριο *to ghramareeo*
grandfather ο παππούς *o papoos*
grandmother η γιαγιά *ee yaya*
grandparents ο παππούς και η γιαγιά *o papoos ke ee yaya*
grapefruit το γκρέιπ-φρουτ *to grapefruit*
grapes τα σταφύλια *ta stafeelya*
grated cheese το τυρί τριμένο *to teeree treemeno*
grater ο τρίφτης *o treeftees*
greasy λιπαρός *leeparos*
great μεγάλος *meghalos*
Greece η Ελλάδα *ee eladha*
Greek (person) ο Έλληνας / η Ελληνίδα *o eleenas / ee eleeneedha*
Greek adj ελληνικός *eleeneekos*
green πράσινος *praseenos*
grey γκρίζος *greezos*

g

grilled της σχάρας *tees skharas*
grocer's το μπακάλικο *to bakaleeko* // το παντοπωλείο *to pandopoleeo*
ground n το έδαφος *to edhafos*
ground adj (coffee, etc.) αλεσμένος *alesmenos*
ground floor το ισόγειο *to eesoyeeo*
groundsheet ο μουσαμάς εδάφους *o moosamas edhafoos*
group η ομάδα *ee omadha*
to grow μεγαλώνω *meghalono*
guarantee η εγγύηση *ee engeeyeesee*
guard (on train) ο υπεύθυνος τρένου *o eepeftheenos trenoo*
guest ο φιλοξενούμενος *o feeloksenoomenos*
guesthouse ο ξενώνας *o ksenonas*
guide ο / η ξεναγός *o / ee ksenaghos*
to guide ξεναγώ *ksenagho*
guidebook ο οδηγός *o odheeghos*
guided tour η περιήγηση με ξεναγό *ee peree-eeyeesee me ksenagho*
gym shoes τα αθλητικά παπούτσια *ta athleeteeka papootsya*

h **H**

haemorrhoids οι αιμορροΐδες *ee emoroeedhes*
hair τα μαλλιά *ta malya*

hairbrush η βούρτσα *ee voortsa*
haircut το κούρεμα *to koorema*
hairdresser ο κομμωτής / η κομμώτρια *o komotees / ee komotreea*
hairdryer το πιστολάκι *to peestolakee*
half το μισό *to meeso*
  half an hour μισή ώρα *meesee ora*
half board (η) ημιδιατροφή *(ee) eemeedheeatrofee*
half-bottle το μικρό μπουκάλι *to meekro bookalee*
half price μισή τιμή *meesee teemee*
ham το ζαμπόν *to zambon*
hamburger το χάμπουργκερ *to khamboorger*
hammer το σφυρί *to sfeeree*
hand το χέρι *to kheree*
handbag η τσάντα *ee tsanda*
handicapped ανάπηρος *anapeeros*
handkerchief το μαντήλι *to mandeelee*
hand luggage οι χειραποσκευή *ee kheeraposkevee*
hand-made χειροποίητος *kheeropee-eetos*
to hang up (phone) κλείνω *kleeno*
to happen συμβαίνω *seemveno*
  what happened? τι συνέβη; *tee seenevee*
happy ευτυχισμένος *efteekheesmenos*
harbour το λιμάνι *to leemanee*
hard (difficult) δύσκολος *dheeskolos*
hard-boiled (egg) σφιχτό *sfeekhto*
hardware shop το σιδηροπωλείο *to seedheeropoleeo*
harvest ο θερισμός *o thereesmos*
hat το καπέλο *to kapelo*
to have see GRAMMAR
hay fever η αλλεργικη ρινίτιδα *ee aleryeekee reeneeteedha*
hazelnut το φουντούκι *to foondookee*
he αυτός *aftos*
head το κεφάλι *to kefalee*
headache: *I have a headache* έχω πονοκέφαλο *ekho ponokefalo*
headlights οι προβολείς του αυτοκινήτου *ee provolees too aftokeeneetoo*
headphones τα ακουστικά *ta akoosteeka*
to hear ακούω *akooo*
hearing aid το ακουστικό βαρηκοΐας *to akoosteeko vareekoeeas*
heart η καρδιά *ee kardhya*
heart attack η καρδιακή προσβολή *ee kardheeakee prosvolee*
heartburn η καούρα *ee kaoora*
heater η θερμάστρα *ee thermastra*
heating η θέρμανση *ee thermansee*
heavy βαρύς *varees*

h

hello γεια σας *ya sas*
helmet ο κράνος *o kranos*
to help βοηθώ *voeetho*
  help! βοήθεια *voeetheea*
hepatitis η ηπατίτιδα *ee eepateeteedha*
herb το βότανο *to votano*
herbal tea το τσάι του βουνού *to tsaee to voonoo*
here εδώ *edho*
hernia η κήλη *ee keelee*
high ψηλός *pseelos*
high blood pressure η ψηλή πίεση *ee pseelee peeyesee*
high chair η ψηλή παιδική καρέκλα *ee pseelee pedheekee karekla*
hill ο λόφος *o lofos*
  (slope) η πλαγιά *ee playa*
hill walking η ορειβασία *ee oreevaseea*
to hire νοικιάζω *neekyazo*
to hit χτυπώ *khteepo*
hitchhike το οτοστόπ *to otostop*
HIV positive θετικός για EITZ *theteekos ya aids*
to hold κρατώ *krato*
hold-up η καθυστέρηση *ee katheestereesee*
hole η τρύπα *ee treepa*

h

holiday οι διακοπές *ee dheeakopes*
home το σπίτι *to speetee*
  at home στο σπίτι *sto speetee*
honey το μέλι *to melee*
honeymoon ο μήνας του μέλιτος *o meenas too meleetos*
hook *(fishing)* το αγκίστρι *to angkeestree*
to hope ελπίζω *elpeezo*
hors d'œuvre τα ορεκτικά *ta orekteeka*
horse το άλογο *to alogho*
hospital το νοσοκομείο *to nosokomeeo*
hot ζεστός *zestos*
  I'm hot ζεσταίνομαι *zestenome*
  it's hot έχει ζέστη *ekhee zestee*
  hot water το ζεστό νερό *to zesto nero*
hotel το ξενοδοχείο *to ksenodhokheeo*
hour η ώρα *ee ora*
house το σπίτι *to speetee*
housewife η νοικοκυρά *ee neekokeera*
house wine το κρασί χύμα *to krasee kheema*

h

how πώς *pos*
  how long? πόση ώρα; *posee ora*
  how much? πόσο; *poso*
  how many? πόσα; *posa*

how are you? πώς είστε; *pos eeste*
hungry: *I'm hungry* πεινώ *peeno*
to hurry: *I'm in a hurry* βιάζομαι *vyazome*
to hurt: *that hurts* με πονά *me pona*
husband ο σύζυγος *o seezeeghos*
hydrofoil το ιπτάμενο δελφίνι *to eeptameno dhelfeenee*
hypodermic needle η υποδερμική βελόνα *ee eepodhermeekee velona*

I

I εγώ *egho*
ice ο πάγος *o paghos*
ice cream / ice lolly το παγωτό *to paghoto*
iced *(drink)* παγωμένος *paghomenos*
icon η εικόνα *ee eekona*
if αν *an*
ignition η ανάφλεξη *ee anafleksee*
ignition key το κλειδί μίζας *to kleedhee meezas*
ill άρρωστος *arostos*
immediately αμέσως *amesos*
immunisation ο εμβολισμός *o emvoleesmos*
important σπουδαίος *spoodheos*
impossible αδύνατο *adheenato*
in μέσα *mesa*
  (with countries, towns) σε **(στο / στη / στο)** *se (sto / stee / sto)*
included συμπεριλαμβάνεται *seembereelamvanete*
indigestion η δυσπεψία *ee dheespepseea*
indoors εσωτερικά *esotereeka*
infectious μεταδοτικός *metadhoteekos*
information οι πληροφορίες *ee pleeroforeeyes*
information office το γραφείο πληροφοριών *to ghrafeeo pleeroforeeon*
inhaler η συσκευή εισπνοής *ee seeskevee eespnoees*
injection η ένεση *ee enesee*
injured τραυματισμένος *travmateesmenos*
ink το μελάνι *to melanee*
inner tube η σαμπρέλα *ee sambrela*
insect το έντομο *to endomo*
insect bite το τσίμπημα *to tseembeema*
insect repellent το εντομοαπωθητικό *to endomoapotheeteeko*
inside *n (interior)* το εσωτερικό *to esotereeko*
  inside the car μέσα στο αυτοκίνητο *mesa sto aftokeeneeto*
  it's inside είναι μέσα *eene mesa*
instant coffee στιγμιαίος καφές *steeghmyeos kafes*
instructor ο εκπαιδευτής *o ekpedheftees*
insulin η ινσουλίνη *ee eensooleenee*

insurance η ασφάλεια *ee asfaleea*
insurance certificate η βεβαίωση ασφαλίσεως *ee veveosee asfaleeseos*
insured ασφαλισμένος *asfaleesmenos*
interesting ενδιαφέρων *endheeaferon*
international διεθνής *dhee-ethnees*
internet το ιντερνέτ *to eenternet*
interpreter ο / η διερμηνέας *o / ee dhee-ermeeneas*
interval *(theatre)* το διάλειμμα *to dheealeema*
into σε (στο / στη / στο) *se (sto / stee / sto)*
invitation η πρόσκληση *ee proskleesee*
to invite προσκαλώ *proskalo*
invoice το τιμολόγιο *to teemoloyo*
Ireland η Ιρλανδία *ee eerlandheea*
Irish *(person)* ο Ιρλανδός / η Ιρλανδή *o eerlandhos / ee eerlandhee*
iron *(for clothes)* το σίδερο *to seedhero*
   (metal) ο σίδηρος *o seedheeros*
to iron σιδερώνω *seedherono*
ironmonger's το σιδηροπωλείο *to seedheeropoleeo*
is *see* **(to be)** GRAMMAR
island το νησί *to neesee*
it το *to*

Italy η Ιταλία *ee eetaleea*
itch η φαγούρα *ee faghoora*
itemised bill ο αναλυτικός λογαριασμός *o analeeteekos logharyasmos*

J

jack ο γρύλος *o ghreelos*
jacket το μπουφάν *to boofan*
jam η μαρμελάδα *ee marmeladha*
jammed στριμωγμένος *streemoghmenos*
jar το βάζο *to vazo*
jaundice ο ίκτερος *o eekteros*
jeans το μπλου τζιν *to bluejean*
jelly το ζελέ *to zele*
jellyfish η τσούχτρα *ee tsookhtra*
jersey η φανέλα *ee fanela*
to jetski το jetski *to jetski*
jetty ο μώλος *o molos*
jeweller's το κοσμηματοπωλείο *to kosmeematopoleeo*
jewellery τα κοσμήματα *ta kosmeemata*
job η δουλειά *ee dhoolya*
to jog κάνω τζόκινγκ *kano jogging*
joint το άρθρο *to arthro*

joke το αστείο *to asteeo*
journey το ταξίδι *to takseedhee*
jug η κανάτα *ee kanata*
juice ο χυμός *o kheemos*
jump leads τα καλώδια μπαταρίας *ta kalodheea batareeas*
junction *(crossroads)* η διασταύρωση *ee dheeastavrosee*
just: *just two* μόνο δύο *mono dheeo*
  I've just arrived μόλις έφτασα *molees eftasa*

k

to keep κρατώ *krato*
kettle ο βραστήρας *o vrasteeras*
key το κλειδί *to kleedhee*
key-ring το μπρελόκ *to brelok*
kid *(meat)* το κατσικάκι *to katseekakee*
kidneys τα νεφρά *ta nefra*
kilo το κιλό *to keelo*
kilometre το χιλιόμετρο *to kheelyometro*
kind *n (sort)* το είδος *to eedhos*
kind *adj* ευγενικός *efyeneekos*
king ο βασιλιάς *o vaseelyas*
kiosk το περίπτερο *to pereeptero*
to kiss φιλώ *feelo*
kitchen η κουζίνα *ee koozeena*
kitchen paper το χαρτί κουζίνας *to khartee koozeenas*
kitten το γατάκι *to ghatakee*
kiwi fruit το ακτινίδο *to akteeneedho*
knee το γόνατο *to ghonato*
knee highs οι κάλτσες *ee kaltses*
knickers *(women's)* η κυλότα *ee keelota*
knife το μαχαίρι *to makheree*
to knock down *(by car)* χτυπώ με αυτοκίνητο *khteepo me aftokeeneeto*
to knock over *(vase, glass)* ρίχνω κάτω *reekhno kato*

L

label η ετικέτα *ee eteeketa*
lace η δαντέλα *ee dhandela*
laces *(of shoe)* τα κορδόνια *ta kordhoneea*
ladder η σκάλα *ee skala*
ladies *(toilet)* Γυναικών *yeenekon*
lady η κυρία *ee keereea*
lager η μπίρα *ee beera*
lake η λίμνη *ee leemnee*

lamb το αρνάκι *to arnakee*
lamp η λάμπα *ee lamba*
to land *(plane)* προσγειώνω *prosyeeono*
landslide η καθίζηση *ee katheezeesee*
language η γλώσσα *ee ghlosa*
laptop το λάπτοπ *to laptop*
large μεγάλος *meghalos*
last τελευταίος *telefteos*
late *(in the day)* αργά *argha*
  I am late *(for an appointment)* έχω αργήσει *ekho aryeesee*
later αργότερα *arghotera*
laundrette το πλυντήριο *to pleendeereeo*
laundry service η υπηρεσία πλυντηρίου *ee eepeereseea pleendeereeoo*
lavatory η τουαλέτα *ee tooaleta*
lawyer ο / η δικηγόρος *o / ee dheekeeghoros*
laxative το καθαρτικό *to katharteeko*
lay-by η βοηθητική λωρίδα *ee voeetheeteekee loreedha*
lazy τεμπέλης *tembelees*
lead *(electric)* το καλώδιο *to kalodheeo*
leader *(guide)* ο / η ξεναγός *o / ee ksenaghos*
leadfree αμόλυβδος *amoleevdhos*
leaf το φύλλο *to feelo*
leak η διαρροή *ee dheearoee*
to learn μαθαίνω *matheno*
least: at least τουλάχιστο *toolakheesto*
leather το δέρμα *to dherma*
leather goods τα δερμάτινα είδη *ta dhermateena eedhee*
to leave *(go away)* φεύγω *fevgho*
leek το πράσσο *to praso*
left: (on/to the) left αριστερά *areestera*
left-luggage *(office)* η φύλαξη αποσκευών *ee feelaksee aposkevon*
leg το πόδι *to podhee*
leggings οι περισκελίδες *ee pereeskeleedhes*
lemon το λεμόνι *to lemonee*
lemonade η λεμονάδα *ee lemonadha*
lemon tea το τσάι με λεμόνι *to tsaee me lemonee*
to lend δανείζω *dhaneezo*
length το μήκος *to meekos*
lens ο φακός *o fakos*
lentils οι φακές *ee fakes*
less: less milk λιγότερο γάλα *leeghotero ghala*
lesson το μάθημα *to matheema*
to let *(allow)* επιτρέπω *epeetrepo*
  (hire out) νοικιάζω *neekyazo*

letter το γράμμα *to ghrama*

letterbox το γραμματοκιβώτιο *to ghramatokeevotyo*

lettuce το μαρούλι *to maroolee*

level crossing η σιδηροδρομική διασταύρωση *ee seedheerodhromeekee dheeastavrosee*

library η βιβλιοθήκη *ee veevleeotheekee*

licence η άδεια *ee adheea*

to lie down ξαπλώνω *ksaplono*

lifeboat η ναυαγοσωστική λέμβος *ee navaghososteekee lemvos*

lifeguard ο ναυαγοσώστης *o navaghosostees*

life insurance η ασφάλεια ζωής *ee asfaleea zoees*

life jacket το σωσίβιο *to soseeveeo*

lift το ασανσέρ *to asanser*

lift pass *(skiing)* το εισιτήριο *to eeseeteereeo*

light το φως *to fos*

light bulb ο γλόμπος *o ghlobos*

lighter *(to light a cigarette)* ο αναπτήρας *o anapteeras*

lightning ο κεραυνός *o keravnos*

to like : I like μου αρέσει *moo aresee*

lilo το φουσκωτό στρώμα *to fooskoto stroma*

lime *(fruit)* το γλυκολέμονο *to ghleekolemono*

line η γραμμή *ee ghramee*

lip reading η χειλοανάγνωση *ee kheeloanaghnosee*

lip salve το προστατευτικό στικ *to prostatefteeko stick*

lipstick το κραγιόν *to krayon*

liqueur το λικέρ *to leeker*

to listen ακούω *akooo*

litre το λίτρο *to leetro*

litter τα σκουπίδια *ta skoopeedhya*

little μικρός *meekros*
  a little λίγο *leegho*

to live μένω *meno*
  he lives in London μένει στο Λονδίνο *menee sto londheeno*

liver το συκώτι *to seekotee*

living room το καθιστικό *to katheesteeko*

lizard η σαύρα *ee savra*

lobster ο αστακός *o astakos*

local τοπικός *topeekos*

lock η κλειδαριά *ee kleedharya*

to lock κλειδώνω *kleedhono*
  I'm locked out κλειδώθηκα έξω *kleedhotheeka ekso*

locker *(luggage)* η θήκη *ee theekee*

log book η άδεια κυκλοφορίας *ee adheea keekloforeeas*

lollipop το γλειφιτζούρι *to ghleefeedzooree*

London το Λονδίνο *to londheeno*
long μακρύς *makrees*
to look at κοιτάζω *keetazo*
to look after φροντίζω *frondeezo*
to look for γυρεύω *yeerevo*
lorry το φορτηγό *to forteegho*
to lose χάνω *khano*
lost χαμένος *khamenos*
  I've lost my wallet έχασα το πορτοφόλι μου *ekhasa to portofolee moo*
  I am lost χάθηκα *khatheeka*
lost-property office το γραφείο απωλεσθέντων αντικειμένων *to ghrafeeo apolesthendon andeekeemenon*
lot: a lot (of) πολύς *polees*
lotion η λοσιόν *ee losyon*
loud δυνατός *dheenatos*
lounge (at airport) η αίθουσα *ee ethoosa*
  (in hotel, house) το σαλόνι *to salonee*
to love αγαπώ *aghapo*
low χαμηλός *khameelos*
low-alcohol beer η μπίρα χαμηλή σε αλκοόλ *ee beera khameelee se alko-ol*
low-fat λάϊτ *laeet*
luggage οι αποσκευές *ee aposkeves*
luggage allowance το επιτρεπόμενο βάρος αποσκευών *to epeetrepomeno varos aposkevon*
luggage rack ο χώρος αποσκευών *o khoros aposkevon*
luggage tag η ετικέτα *ee eteeketa*
luggage trolley το καροτσάκι αποσκευών *to karotsakee aposkevon*
lump η εξόγκωση *ee eksogosee*
lunch το μεσημεριανό *to meseemereeano*
lung ο πνεύμονας *o pnevmonas*
luxury η πολυτέλεια *ee poleeteleea*

M

machine η μηχανή *ee meekhanee*
mad τρελός *trelos*
magazine το περιοδικό *to pereeodheeko*
magnifying glass ο μεγενθυτικός φακός *o meyentheeteekos fakos*
maiden name το πατρώνυμο *to patroneemo*
main course (of meal) το κύριο πιάτο *to keereeo pyato*
mains (electric) ο κεντρικός αγωγός *o kendreekos aghoghos*
to make κάνω *kano*
make-up το μακιγιάζ *to makeeyaz*
male αρσενικός *arseneekos*
man (mankind) ο άνθρωπος *o anthropos*

116

(as opposed to woman) **ο άντρας** *o andras*

manager ο διαχειριστής *o dheeakheereestees*

many πολλοί *polee*
  many people πολλοί άνθρωποι *polee anthropee*

map ο χάρτης *o khartees*

marble το μάρμαρο *to marmaro*

margarine η μαργαρίνη *ee marghareenee*

marina η μαρίνα *ee mareena*

market η αγορά *ee aghora*

market day η μέρα της αγοράς *ee mera tees aghoras*

marmalade η μαρμελάδα *ee marmeladha*

marriage certificate το πιστοποιητικό γάμου *to peestopyeeteeko ghamoo*

married παντρεμένος *pandremenos*

mass *(in church)* η Θεία Λειτουργία *ee theea leetooryeea*

match *(game)* ο αγώνας *o aghonas*

matches τα σπίρτα *ta speerta*

material το υλικό *to eeleeko*

matter: it doesn't matter δεν πειράζει *dhen peerazee*
  what's the matter with you? τι έχεις; *tee ekhees*

mayonnaise η μαγιονέζα *ee mayoneza*

meal το γεύμα *to yevma*

to mean εννοώ *eno-o*

measles η ιλαρά *ee eelara*

meat το κρέας *to kreas*

mechanic ο μηχανικός *o meekhaneekos*

medicine *(drug)* το φάρμακο *to farmako*

Mediterranean η Μεσόγειος *ee mesoyeeos*

medium *(wine)* μέτριο γλυκύ *metreeo ghleekee*
  (steak, size) μέτριο *metreeo*

to meet συναντώ *seenando*

meeting η συνάντηση *ee seenandeesee*

melon το πεπόνι *to peponee*
  (watermelon) το καρπούζι *to karpoozee*

member *(of club)* το μέλος *to melos*

men οι άντρες *ee andres*

menu ο κατάλογος *o kataloghos* // το μενού *to menoo*

message το μήνυμα *to meeneema*

metal το μέταλλο *to metalo*

meter ο μετρητής *o metreetees*

metre το μέτρο *to metro*

microwave *(oven)* ο φούρνος μικροκυμάτων *o foornos meekrokeematon*

midday το μεσημέρι *to meseemeree*

midnight τα μεσάνυχτα *ta mesaneekhta*

117

m

migraine η ημικρανία *ee eemeekraneea*

mile το μίλι *to meelee*

milk το γάλα *to ghala*

milkshake το μιλκσέικ *to meelkseyk*

millimetre το χιλιοστόμετρο *to kheelyostometro*

million το εκατομμύριο *to ekatomeereeo*

mince ο κιμάς *o keemas*

to mind: *do you mind if...?* σας ενοχλεί αν...; *sas enokhlee an...*

mineral water το επιτραπέζιο νερό *to epeetrapezeeo nero*
    (sparkling) το αεριούχο μεταλλικό νερό *to aeryookho metaleeko nero*

minimum ελάχιστος *elakheestos*

minor road ο δευτερεύων δρόμος *o dhefterevon dhromos*

mint *(herb)* ο δυόσμος *o dheeosmos*

minute το λεπτό *to lepto*

mirror ο καθρέφτης *o kathreftees*

to miss *(train, etc.)* χάνω *khano*

Miss η Δεσποινίς *ee dhespeenees*

missing χαμένος *khamenos*

mistake το λάθος *to lathos*

misunderstanding η παρεξήγηση *ee parekseeyeesee*

mobile phone το κινητό τηλέφωνο *to keeneeto teelefono*

moisturizer η υδατική κρέμα *ee eedhateekee krema*

monastery το μοναστήρι *to monasteeree*

money τα χρήματα *ta khreemata* // τα λεφτά *ta lefta*

money order η ταχυδρομική επιταγή *ee takheedhromeekee epeetayee*

month ο μήνας *o meenas*

monument το μνημείο *to mneemeeo*

moon το φεγγάρι *to fengaree*

more περισσότερο *pereesotero*
    more bread κι άλλο ψωμί *kee alo psomee*

morning το πρωί *to proee*

mosaic το μωσαϊκό *to mosaeeko*

mosque το τζαμί *to dzamee*

mosquito το κουνούπι *to koonoopee*

most το περισσότερο *to pereesotero*

moth η πεταλουδίτσα *ee petaloodheetsa*

mother η μητέρα *ee meetera*

mother-in-law η πεθερά *ee pethera*

motor η μηχανή *ee meekhanee*

motorbike η μοτοσικλέτα *ee motoseekleta*

motorboat η βενζινάκατος *ee venzeenakatos*

motorway ο αυτοκινητόδρομος *o aftokeeneetodhromos*

mountain το βουνό *to voono*

mouse το ποντίκι *to pondeekee*

mousse το μους *to moos*
moustache το μουστάκι *to moostakee*
mouth το στόμα *to stoma*
to move κινούμαι *keenoome*
Mr Κύριος *keereeos*
Mrs Κυρία *keereea*
much πολύς *polees*
  too much πάρα πολύ *para polee*
  very much πάρα πολύ *para polee*
mumps οι μαγουλάδες *ee maghooladhes*
muscle ο μυς *o mees*
museum το μουσείο *to mooseeo*
mushroom το μανιτάρι *to maneetaree*
music η μουσική *ee mooseekee*
mussel το μύδι *to meedhee*
must: *I must go* πρέπει να πάω *prepee na pao*
  you must go πρέπει να πας *prepee na pas*
  he / she must go πρέπει να πάει *prepee na paee*
  we must go πρέπει να πάμε *prepee na pame*
mustard η μουστάρδα *ee moostardha*

N

nail *(metal)* το καρφί *to karfee*
  (on finger, toe) το νύχι *to neekhee*
nail polish το βερνίκι νυχιών *to verneekee neekhyon*
nail polish remover το ασετόν *to aseton*
nailbrush η βούρτσα των νυχιών *ee voortsa ton neekhyon*
naked γυμνός *yeemnos*
name το όνομα *to onoma*
napkin η πετσέτα *ee petseta*
nappy η πάνα *ee pana*
narrow στενός *stenos*
nationality η υπηκοότητα *ee eepeeko-oteeta*
navy blue μπλε *ble*
near κοντά *konda*
necessary απαραίτητος *apareteetos*
neck ο λαιμός *o lemos*
necklace το κολιέ *to kolye*
to need: *I need ...* χρειάζομαι ... *khreeazome ...*
needle η βελόνα *ee velona*
  a needle and thread βελόνα και κλωστή *velona ke klostee*
negative *(photography)* αρνητικός *arneeteekos*
neighbour ο γείτονας / η γειτόνισσα *o yeetonas / ee yeetoneesa*
nephew ο ανιψιός *o aneepsyos*

119

n

never ποτέ pote
  I never go there δεν πηγαίνω ποτέ εκεί dhen peeyeno pote ekee
new καινούριος kenooryos
news *(TV, radio)* οι ειδήσεις ee eedheesees
newspaper η εφημερίδα ee efeemereedha
New Year: *happy New Year!* καλή χρονιά! kalee khronya
New Zealand η Νέα Ζηλανδία ee nea zeelandheea
next επόμενος epomenos
nice *(thing)* ωραίος oreos
  (person) καλός kalos
niece η ανιψιά ee aneepsya
night η νύχτα ee neekhta
nightclub το νυχτερινό κέντρο to neekhtereeno kendro
nightdress το νυχτικό to neekhteeko
no όχι okhee
nobody κανένας kanenas
noisy θορυβώδης thoreevodhees
non-alcoholic μη οινοπνευματώδης mee eenopnevmatodhees
none κανένα kanena
non-smoking μη καπνίζοντες mee kapneezondes
north ο βορράς o voras
Nothern Ireland η Βόρεια Ιρλανδία ee voreea eerlandheea

n

nose η μύτη ee meetee
not μη mee
  I am not δεν είμαι dhen eeme
note *(banknote)* το χαρτονόμισμα to khartonomeesma
  (letter) το σημείωμα to seemeeoma
note pad το σημειωματάριο to seemeeomatareeo
nothing τίποτα teepota
now τώρα tora
nudist beach η παραλία γυμνιστών ee paraleea yeemneeston
number ο αριθμός o areethmos
number plate η πινακίδα κυκλοφορίας ee peenakeedha keekloforeeas
nurse η νοσοκόμα ee nosokoma
nut *(peanut)* το φιστίκι to feesteekee
  (walnut) το καρύδι to kareedhee
  (hazelnut) το φουντούκι to foondookee
  (for bolt) το παξιμάδι to pakseemadhee

O

oar το κουπί to koopee
occasionally κάπου-κάπου kapoo-kapoo
octopus το χταπόδι to khtapodhee
odd number ο μονός αριθμός o monos areethmos

of: *of course* βέβαια *vevea*

off *(light, machine, etc.)* σβυστός *sveestos*
  it's off (rotten) είναι χαλασμένο *eene khalasmeno*

to offer προσφέρω *prosfero*

office το γραφείο *to ghrafeeo*

often συχνά *seekhna*

oil το λάδι *to ladhee*

oil filter το φίλτρο του λαδιού *to feeltro too ladhyoo*

ointment η αλοιφή *ee aleefee*

OK εντάξει *endaksee*

old *(person)* ηλικιωμένος *eeleekyomenos*
  (thing) παλιός *palyos*
  how old are you? πόσων χρονών είστε; *poson khronon eeste*

olive oil το ελαιόλαδο *to eleoladho*

olives οι ελιές *ee elyes*

omelette η ομελέτα *ee omeleta*

on *(light, radio, TV)* ανοιχτός *aneekhtos*
  on the table στο τραπέζι *sto trapezee*

once μία φορά *meea fora*

one ένας / μία / ένα *enas (masculine) / meea (feminine) / ena (neuter)*

one-way *(street)* ο μονόδρομος *o monodhromos*
  (ticket) το απλό εισιτήριο *to aplo eeseeteereeo*

onion το κρεμμύδι *to kremeedhee*

only μόνο *mono*

to open ανοίγω *aneegho*

open *adj* ανοικτός *aneektos*

operator *(telephone)* η τηλεφωνήτρια *ee teelefoneetreea*

opposite απέναντι *apenandee*

or ή *ee*

orange *(fruit)* το πορτοκάλι *to portokalee*
  (colour) πορτοκαλί *portokalee*

orange juice ο χυμός πορτοκαλιού *o kheemos portokalyoo*

orchard το περιβόλι *to pereevolee*

to order παραγγέλλω *parangelo*

organize οργανώνω *orghanono*

original αρχικός *arkheekos*

Orthodox *(religion)* ορθόδοξος *orthodhoksos*

other άλλος *alos*

out *(light, etc.)* σβησμένος *sveesmenos*
  he's out λείπει *leepee*

outdoors στην ύπαιθρο *steen eepethro*

outside έξω *ekso*

outskirts τα περίχωρα *ta pereekhora*

oven ο φούρνος *o foornos*

121

o

over πάνω από pano apo
over there εκεί πέρα ekee pera
to owe: you owe me μου χρωστάς moo khrostas
owner ο ιδιοκτήτης o eedheeokteetees
oxygen το οξυγόνο to okseeghono
oyster το στρείδι to streedhee

P

to pack πακετάρω paketaro
package το δέμα to dhema
package tour η οργανωμένη εκδρομή ee orghanomenee ekdhromee
packet το πακέτο to paketo
paddling pool η λιμνούλα για παιδιά ee leemnoola ya pedhya
padlock το λουκέτο to looketo
paid πληρωμένος pleeromenos
painful οδυνηρός odheeneeros
painkiller το παυσίπονο to pafseepono
painting ο πίνακας o peenakas
pair το ζευγάρι to zevgharee
palace το παλάτι to palatee
pale χλομός khlomos
pan η κατσαρόλα ee katsarola
pancake η κρέπα ee krepa
panties η κυλότα ee keelota
pants (underpants) το σώβρακο to sovrako
paper το χαρτί to khartee
parcel το δέμα to dhema
pardon παρακαλώ parakalo
I beg your pardon με συγχωρείτε me seenkhoreete
parents οι γονείς o ghonees
park n το πάρκο to parko
to park (in car) παρκάρω parkaro
parsley ο μαϊντανός o maeendanos
part το μέρος to meros
party (group) η ομάδα ee omadha
(celebration) το πάρτυ to party
passenger ο επιβάτης o epeevatees
passport το διαβατήριο to dheeavateereeo
passport control ο έλεγχος διαβατηρίων o elengkhos dheeavateereeon
pasta τα ζυμαρικά ta zeemareeka
pastry η ζύμη ee zeemee
(cake) το γλύκισμα to ghleekeesma
path το μονοπάτι to monopatee
pavement το πεζοδρόμιο to pezodhromeeo

to pay πληρώνω *pleerono*

payment η πληρωμή *ee pleeromee*

peach το ροδάκινο *to rodhakeeno*

peak hour η ώρα αιχμής *ee ora ekhmees*

peanut το φιστίκι *to feesteekee*

pear το αχλάδι *to akhladhee*

peas οι αρακάδες *ee arakades*

pebble το πετραδάκι *to petradhakee*

pedestrian (person) ο πέζος / η πεζή *o pezos / ee pezee*

pedestrian crossing η διασταύρωση πεζών *ee dheeastavrosee pezon*

to peel ξεφλουδίζω *ksefloodheezo*

peg (for tent) ο πάσσαλος *o pasalos*
(for clothes) το μανταλάκι *to mandalakee*

pen το στύλο *to steelo*

pencil το μολύβι *to moleevee*

penicillin η πενικιλλίνη *ee peneekeeleenee*

penknife ο σουγιάς *o sooyas*

pensioner ο / η συνταξιούχος *o / ee seendaksyookhos*

pepper (spice) το πιπέρι *to peeperee*
(vegetable) η πιπεριά *ee peeperya*

per: *per hour* την ώρα *teen ora*

perfect τέλειος *teleeos*

performance η παράσταση *ee parastasee*

perfume το άρωμα *to aroma*

perhaps ίσως *eesos*

period (menstruation) η περίοδος *ee pereeodhos*

perm η περμανάντ *ee permanand*

permit άδεια *adheea*

person το πρόσωπο *to prosopo*

personal stereo το προσωπικό στερεοφωνικό *to prosopeeko stereofoneeko*

pet το κατικοίδιο ζώο *to kateekeedhyo zo-o*

petrol η βενζίνη *ee venzeenee*

petrol station το βενζινάδικο *to venzeenadheeko //* το πρατήριο βενζίνης *to prateereeo venzeenees*

phone *see* **telephone**

phonecard η τηλεκάρτα *ee teelekarta*

photocopy η φωτοτυπία *ee fototeepeea*

photograph η φωτογραφία *ee fotoghrafeea*

phrase book το βιβλιαράκι φράσεων *to veevleearakee fraseon*

picture η εικόνα *ee eekona*

pie η πίτα *ee peeta*

piece το κομμάτι *to komatee*

pier η αποβάθρα *ee apovathra*

pill το χάπι *to khapee*
pillow το μαξιλάρι *to makseelaree*
pillowcase η μαξιλαροθήκη *ee makseelarotheekce*
pin η καρφίτσα *ee karfeetsa*
pine το πεύκο *to pefko*
pineapple ο ανανάς *o ananas*
pink ροζ *roz*
pipe η πίπα *ee peepa*
pistachio nut το φυστίκι Αιγίνης *to feesteekee eyeenees*
plaster *(for broken limb)* ο γύψος *o yeepsos*
plastic πλαστικός *plasteekos*
plate το πιάτο *to pyato*
platform η αποβάθρα *ee apovathra*
to play παίζω *pezo*
playroom το δωμάτιο των παιδιών *to dhomateeo ton pedhyon*
please παρακαλώ *parakalo*
pleased ευχαριστημένος *efkhareesteemenos*
pliers η πένσα *ee pensa*
plug *(electric)* η πρίζα *ee preeza*
plum η βανίλια *ee vaneelya*
plumber ο υδραυλικός *o eedhravleekos*

poisonous δηλητηριώδης *dheeleeteereeodhees*
police η αστυνομία *ee asteenomeea*
policeman ο αστυνόμος *o asteenomos*
police station το αστυνομικό τμήμα *to asteenomeeko tmeema*
polish *(for shoes)* το βερνίκι *to verneekee*
polluted μολυσμένος *moleesmenos*
pollution η ρύπανση *ee reepansee*
pony trekking η ιππασία *ee eepaseea*
pool *(for swimming)* η πισίνα *ee peeseena*
popular δημοφιλής *dheemofeelees*
  (fashionable) **κοσμικός** *kosmeekos*
pork το χοιρινό *to kheereeno*
port *(harbour)* το λιμάνι *to leemanee*
porter ο αχθοφόρος *o akhthoforos*
possible δυνατός *dheenatos*
to post *(letter)* ταχυδρομώ *takheedhromo*
postbox το ταχυδρομικό κουτί *to takheedhromeeko kootee*
postcard η καρτποστάλ *ee kartpostal*

postcode ο κωδικός *o kodheekos*
post office το ταχυδρομείο *to takheedhromeeo*
pot η κατσαρόλα *ee katsarola*
potato η πατάτα *ee patata*

pottery τα κεραμικά *to kerameeka*
pound *(money)* η λίρα *ee leera*
powdered milk το γάλα σε σκόνη *to ghala se skonee*
pram το καροτσάκι *to karotsakee*
prawn η γαρίδα *ee ghareedha*
to prefer προτιμώ *proteemo*
pregnant έγγυος *engeeos*
to prepare ετοιμάζω *eteemazo*
prescription η συνταγή *ee seendayee*
present *(gift)* το δώρο *to dhoro*
pretty ωραίος *oreos*
price η τιμή *ee teemee*
price list ο τιμοκατάλογος *o teemokataloghos*
priest ο παπάς *o papas*
private ιδιωτικός *eedheeoteekos*
prize το βραβείο *to vraveeo*
probably πιθανώς *peethanos*
problem το πρόβλημα *to provleema*
programme το πρόγραμμα *to proghrama*
prohibited απαγορευμένος *apaghorevmenos*
to pronounce προφέρω *profero*
　how do you pronounce this? πώς το προφέρετε; *pos to proferete*
Protestant διαμαρτυρόμενος *dheeamarteeromenos*
prune το δαμάσκηνο *to dhamaskeeno*
public δημόσιος *dheemoseeos*
public holiday η γιορτή *ee yortee*
to pull τραβώ *travo*
pullover το πουλόβερ *to poolover*
puncture το τρύπημα *to treepeema*
purple πορφυρός *porfeeros*
purse το τσαντάκι *to tsandakee*
to push σπρώχνω *sprokhno*
push chair το καροτσάκι (μωρού) *to karotsakee (moroo)*
to put βάζω *vazo*
　to put down βάζω κάτω *vazo kato*
pyjamas οι πιζάμες *ee peezames*

Q

quality η ποιότητα *ee peeoteeta*
quay η προκυμαία *ee prokeemea*
queen η βασίλισσα *ee vaseeleesa*
question η ερώτηση *ee eroteesee*
queue η ουρά *ee oora*

quick γρήγορος *ghreeghoros*
quickly γρήγορα *ghreeghora*
quiet ήσυχος *eeseekhos*
quilt *(duvet)* το πάπλωμα *to paploma*

R

rabbit το κουνέλι *to koonelee*
rabies η λύσσα *ee leesa*
racket η ρακέτα *ee raketa*
radiator το καλοριφέρ *to kaloreefer*
radio το ραδιόφωνο *to radheeofono*
radish το ραπανάκι *to rapanakee*
railway station ο σιδηροδρομικός σταθμός *o seedheerodhromeekos stathmos*
rain η βροχή *ee vrokhee*
raincoat το αδιάβροχο *to adheeavrokho*
raining: *it's raining* βρέχει *vrekhee*
raisin η σταφίδα *ee stafeedha*
rare σπάνιος *spanyos*
  (steak) μισοψημένος *meesopseemenos*
rash *(skin)* το εξάνθημα *to eksantheema*
raspberries τα βατόμουρα *ta vatomoora*

rat ο αρουραίος *o arooreos*
rate ο ρυθμός *o reethmos*
  rate of exchange η ισοτιμία *ee eesoteemeea*
raw ωμός *omos*
razor το ξυραφάκι *to kseerafakee*
razor blade το ξυράφι *to kseerafee*
to read διαβάζω *dheeavazo*
ready έτοιμος *eteemos*
real πραγματικός *praghmateekos*
reason ο λόγος *o loghos*
receipt η απόδειξη *ee apodheeksee*
recently τελευταία *teleftea*
reception *(desk)* η ρεσεψιόν *ee resepsyon*
recipe η συνταγή *ee seendayee*
to recommend συνιστώ *seeneesto*
record *(music, etc.)* ο δίσκος *o dheeskos*
red κόκκινος *kokeenos*
reduction η έκπτωση *ee ekptosee*

refill το ανταλλακτικό *to andalakteeko*
refund η επιστροφή χρημάτων *ee epeestrofee khreematon*
registered *(letter)* συστημένο *seesteemeno*
regulations οι κανονισμοί *ee kanoneesmee*

to reimburse αποζημιώνω *apozeemeeono*

relations *(family)* οι συγγενείς *ee seengenees*

to relax ξεκουράζομαι *ksekoorazome*

reliable *(person)* αξιόπιστος *akseeopeestos*
  (car, method) δοκιμασμένος *dhokeemasmenos*

to remain απομένω *apomeno*

to remember θυμάμαι *theemame*

to rent νοικιάζω *neekyazo*

rental το νοίκι *to neekee*

to repair επιδιορθώνω *epeedheeorthono*

to repeat επαναλαμβάνω *epanalamvano*

reservation η κράτηση *ee krateesee*

to reserve κρατώ *krato*

reserved κρατημένος *krateemenos*

rest ξεκούραση *ksekoorasee*
  the rest οι υπόλοιποι *ee eepoleepee*

to rest ξεκουράζομαι *ksekoorazome*

restaurant το εστιατόριο *to esteeatoreeo*

restaurant car το βαγόνι ρεστωράν *to vaghonee restoran*

to retire βγαίνω στη σύνταξη *vyeno stee seendaksee*

retired συνταξιούχος *seendaksyookhos*

to return *(go back, give back)* επιστρέφω *epeestrefo*

return ticket το εισιτήριο με επιστροφή *to eeseeteereeo me epeestrofee*

reverse-charge call κλήση πληρωτέα από τον παραλήπτη *kleesee pleerotea apo ton paraleeptee*

rheumatism οι ρευματισμοί *ee revmateesmee*

rice το ρύζι *to reezee*

rich *(person, food)* πλούσιος *plooseeos*

riding *(equestrian)* η ιππασία *ee eepaseea*

right *(correct, accurate)* σωστός *sostos*
  (on/to the) right δεξιά *dheksya*

ring το δαχτυλίδι *to dhakhteeleedhee*

ripe ώριμος *oreemos*

river το ποτάμι *to potamee*

road ο δρόμος *o dhromos*

road map ο οδικός χάρτης *o odheekos khartees*

roast το ψητό *to pseeto*

to rob ληστεύω *leestevo*

roll *(of bread)* το ψωμάκι *to psomakee*

roof η στέγη *ee steyee*

roof rack η σχάρα *ee skhara*

room *(in house, etc.)* το δωμάτιο *to dhomateeo*
  (space) ο χώρος *o khoros*

room service η υπηρεσία δωματίου *ee eepereseea dhomateeoo*

127

r

rope το σχοινί *to skheenee*

rosé ροζέ *roze*

rotten *(fruit)* χαλασμένος *khalasmenos*

rough *(sea)* τρικυμισμένη *treekeemeesmenee*

round *(shape)* στρογγυλός *strongeelos*
  round Greece γύρω στην Ελλάδα *yeero steen eladha*
  round the corner στη γωνία *stee ghoneea*

route ο δρόμος *o dhromos*

to row *(boat)* κάνω κουπί *kano koopee*

rowing boat η βάρκα με κουπιά *ee varka me koopya*

royal βασιλικός *vaseeleekos*

rubber το λάστιχο *to lasteekho*

rubber band το λαστιχάκι *to lasteekhakee*

rubbish τα σκουπίδια *ta skoopeedhya*

rucksack το σακίδιο *to sakeedheeo*

ruins τα ερείπια *ta ereepya*

rum το ρούμι *to roomee*

to run τρέχω *trekho*

rush hour η ώρα αιχμής *ee ora ekhmees*

rusty σκουριασμένος *skooryasmenos*

S

s

sad λυπημένος *leepeemenos*

safe *adj (medicine)* αβλαβής *avlavees*
  (beach) ακίνδυνος *akeendheenos*

safe *n* το χρηματοκιβώτιο *to khreematokeevotyo*

safety pin η παραμάνα *ee paramana*

sailing η ιστιοπλοΐα *ee eesteeoploeea*

salad η σαλάτα *ee salata*

salad dressing το λαδολέμονο *to ladholemono*

sale *(in shop)* το ξεπούλημα *to ksepooleema*

salmon ο σολομός *o solomos*

salt το αλάτι *to alatee*

same ίδιος *eedheeos*

sand η άμμος *ee amos*

sandals τα πέδιλα *ta pedheela*

sandwich το σάντουϊτς *to sandwich*

sanitary towel η σερβιέτα *ee servyeta*

sardine η σαρδέλα *ee sardhela*

sauce η σάλτσα *ee saltsa*

saucepan η κατσαρόλα *ee katsarola*

saucer το πιατάκι *to pyatakee*

sausage το λουκάνικο *to lookaneeko*

savoury πικάντικος *peekandeekos*

128

to say λέω *leo*

scarf *(long)* το κασκόλ *to kaskol*
  (square) το μαντήλι *to mandeelee*

school το σχολείο *to skholeeo*
  (for 12- to 15-year-olds) το γυμνάσιο *to yeemnaseeo*
  (for 15- to 18- year-olds) το λύκειο *to leekeeo*

scissors το ψαλίδι *to psaleedhee*

Scotland η Σκωτία *ee skoteea*

Scottish *(person)* ο Σκωτσέζος / η Σκωτσέζα *o skotsezos / ee skotseza*

screw η βίδα *ee veedha*

screwdriver το κατσαβίδι *to katsaveedhee*

sculpture το γλυπτό *to ghleepto*

sea η θάλασσα *ee thalasa*

seafood τα θαλασσινά *ta thalaseena*

seasickness η ναυτία *ee nafteea*

seaside η θάλασσα ~~ee thalasa~~ // η παραλία *ee paraleea*

seat *(in theatre)* η θέση *ee thesee*
  (in car, etc.) το κάθισμα *to katheesma*

second δεύτερος *dhefteros*

second class *(ticket, etc.)* δεύτερη θέση *dhefteree thesee*

second-hand μεταχειρισμένος *metakheereesmenos*

to see βλέπω *vlepo*

self-service το σελφ σέρβις *to self service*

to sell πουλώ *poolo*

Sellotape ® το σελοτέιπ *to seloteyp*

send στέλνω *stelno*

separate χωριστός *khoreestos*

serious σοβαρός *sovaros*

to serve σερβίρω *serveero*

service *(in restaurant, etc.)* η εξυπηρέτηση *ee ekseepeereteesee*

service charge το ποσοστό υπηρεσίας *to pososto eepeereseeas*

set menu το καθορισμένο μενού *to kathoreesmeno menoo*

several διάφοροι *dheeaforee*

to sew ράβω *ravo*

shade η σκιά *ee skeea*

shallow ρηχός *reekhos*

shampoo το σαμπουάν *to sambooan*

shampoo and set λούσιμο και στέγνωμα *looseemo ke steghnoma*

to share μοιράζω *meerazo*

to shave ξυρίζομαι *kseereezome*

shaving cream η κρέμα ξυρίσματος *ee krema kseereesmatos*

she αυτή *aftee*

sheep το πρόβατο *to provato*

sheet το σεντόνι *to sendonee*

S

shellfish τα όστρακα *ta ostraka*

ship το πλοίο *to pleeo*

shirt το πουκάμισο *to pookameeso*

shock absorber το αμορτισέρ *to amorteeser*

shoe το παπούτσι *to papootsee*

to shop ψωνίζω *psoneezo*

shop το μαγαζί *to maghazee*

shop assistant (woman) η πωλήτρια *ee poleetreea*
(man) ο πωλητής *o poleetees*

short κοντός *kondos*

short cut ο συντομότερος δρόμος *o seendomoteros dhromos*

shorts το σορτς *to shorts*

show n (in theatre, etc.) η παράσταση *ee parastasee*

to show δείχνω *dheekhno*

shower (in bath) το ντους *to doos*
(rain) η μπόρα *ee bora*

shrimp η γαρίδα *ee ghareedha*

shut (closed) κλειστός *kleestos*

to shut κλείνω *kleeno*

shutters τα παντζούρια *ta pantzooreea*

sick (ill) άρρωστος *arostos*
to be sick (vomit) κάνω εμετό *kano emeto*

S

sightseeing: to go sightseeing επισκέπτομαι τα αξιοθέατα *epeeskeptome ta akseeotheata*

sign (roadsign, notice, etc.) η πινακίδα *ee peenakeedha*

signature η υπογραφή *ee eepoghrafee*

silk το μετάξι *to metaksee*

silver ασημένιος *aseemeneeos*

similar παρόμοιος *paromeeos*

simple απλός *aplos*

to sing τραγουδώ *traghoodho*

single (not married) ελεύθερος *eleftheros*
(not double) μονός *monos*

single bed το μονό κρεββάτι *to mono krevatee*

single room το μονόκλινο δωμάτιο *to monokleeno dhomateeo*

sink ο νεροχύτης *o nerokheetees*

sister η αδελφή *ee adhelfee*

to sit (down) κάθομαι *kathome*

size (of clothes, shoes) το μέγεθος *to meyethos*

ski τα σκι *ta skee*

S

to ski κάνω σκι *kano skee*

ski jacket το μπουφάν του σκι *to boofan too skee*

ski pants το παντελόνι του σκι *to pandelonee too skee*

ski pole το ραβδί του σκι *to ravdhee too skee*

ski run η διαδρομή του σκι *ee dheeadhrom**ee** too sk**ee***

ski suit τα ρούχα του σκι *ta r**oo**kha too sk**ee***

skimmed milk το αποβουτυρωμένο γάλα *to apovooteerom**e**no gh**a**la*

skin το δέρμα *to dh**e**rma*

skin diving το υποβρύχιο κολύμπι *to eepovr**ee**kheeo kol**ee**mbee*

skirt η φούστα *ee f**oo**sta*

sky ο ουρανός *o oor**a**nos*

to sleep κοιμούμαι *keem**oo**me*

sleeper το βαγκόν-λι *to vag**o**n-lee*

sleeping bag το υπνόσακος *o eepn**o**sakos*

sleeping pill το υπνωτικό χάπι *to eepnoteek**o** kh**a**pee*

slice η φέτα *ee f**e**ta*

slide *(photography)* το σλάιντ *to slide*

slippery γλιστερός *ghleester**o**s*

slow σιγά *seegh**a***

small μικρός *meekr**o**s*

smaller (than) μικρότερος (από) *meekr**o**teros (ap**o**)*

smell η μυρωδιά *ee meerodhy**a***

smile το χαμόγελο *to kham**o**yelo*

to smile χαμογελώ *khamoyel**o***

smoke ο καπνός *o kapn**o**s*

to smoke καπνίζω *kapn**ee**zo*

smoked καπνιστός *kapneest**o**s*

snack bar το σνακ μπαρ *to snack bar*

snake το φίδι *to f**ee**dhee*

snorkel ο αναπνευστήρας *o anapnevst**ee**ras*

snow το χιόνι *to khy**o**nee*

snowed up αποκλεισμένος από το χιόνι *apokleesm**e**nos ap**o** to khy**o**nee*

snowing: *it's snowing* χιονίζει *khyon**ee**zee*

so γι'αυτό *yee aft**o***
  so much τόσο πολύ *t**o**so pol**ee***
  so pretty τόσο ωραίος *t**o**so or**e**os*
  so that για να *ya na*

soap το σαπούνι *to sap**oo**nee*

soap powder το απορρυπαντικό *to aporeepandeek**o***

sober ξεμέθυστος *ksem**e**theestos*

sock η κάλτσα *ee k**a**ltsa*

socket *(electrical)* η πρίζα *ee pr**ee**za*

soda *(water)* η σόδα *ee s**o**dha*

soft μαλακός *malak**o**s*

soft drink το αναψυκτικό *to anapseekteek**o***

some μερικοί *mereek**ee***

someone κάποιος *k**a**pyos*

something κάτι *k**a**tee*

S

sometimes κάποτε *kapote*

son ο γιος *o yos*

song το τραγούδι *to traghoodhee*

soon σύντομα *seendoma*
  as soon as possible το συντομότερο *to seendomotero*
  sooner νωρίτερα *noreetera*

sore: it's sore πονάει *ponaee*

sorry: I'm sorry (apology) συγγνώμη *seeghnomee*
  (regret) λυπούμαι *leepoome*

sort το είδος *to eedhos*

soup η σούπα *ee soopa*

south ο νότος *o notos*

souvenir το σουβενίρ *to sooveneer*

space (room) ο χώρος *o khoros*

spanner το κλειδί *to kleedhee*

spare wheel η ρεζέρβα *ee rezerva*

spark plug το μπουζί *to boozee*

sparkling (wine) αφρώδης *afrodhees*

to speak μιλώ *meelo*

special ειδικός *eedheekos*

speciality (in restaurant) η σπεσιαλιτέ *ee spesyaleete*

S

speed η ταχύτητα *ee takheeteeta*

speed limit το όριο ταχύτητας *to oreeo takheeteetas*

spell γράφω *ghrafo*
  how do you spell it? πώς γράφεται; *pos ghrafete*

spicy πικάντικος *peekandeekos*

spinach το σπανάκι *to spanakee*

spirits τα οινοπνευματώδη ποτά *ta eenopnevmatodhee pota*

sponge το σφουγγάρι *to sfoongaree*

spoon το κουτάλι *to kootalee*

sport το σπορ *to spor*

spring (season) η άνοιξη *ee aneeksee*

square (in town) η πλατεία *ee plateea*

squash (sport) το σκουός *to skooos*
  orange squash η πορτοκαλάδα *ee portokaladha*
  lemon squash η λεμονάδα *ee lemonadha*

squid το καλαμάρι *to kalamaree*

stadium το στάδιο *to stadheeo*

stairs η σκάλα *ee skala*

stalls (in theatre) η πλατεία *ee plateea*

S

stamp το γραμματόσημο *to ghramatoseemo*

star (in sky) το άστρο *to astro*

to start αρχίζω *arkheezo*

starter (in meal) το ορεκτικό *to orekteeko*

station ο σταθμός *o stathmos*

stationer's το χαρτοπωλείο *to khartopoleeo*

to stay μένω *meno*

steak το μπιφτέκι *to beeftekee*

steep ανηφορικός *aneeforeekos*

sterling η αγγλική λίρα *ee angleekee leera*

steward *(on a ship)* ο καμαρότος *o kamarotos*
  (on plane) ο αεροσυνοδός *o aeroseenodhos*

stewardess *(on plane)* η αεροσυνοδός *ee aeroseenodhos*

sticking plaster ο λευκοπλάστης *o lefkoplastees*

still *(yet)* ακόμα *akoma*
  (immobile) ακίνητος *akeeneetos*
  (water) μη αεριούχο *mee aeryookho*

sting το τσίμπημα *to tseembeema*

stockings οι κάλτσες *ee kaltses*

stomach το στομάχι *to stomakhee*

stomach upset η στομαχική διαταραχή *ee stomakheekee dheeatarakhee*

to stop σταματώ *stamato*

storm η καταιγίδα *ee kateyeedha*

straight: straight on ευθεία *eftheea*

straw *(for drinking)* το καλαμάκι *to kalamakee*

strawberry η φράουλα *ee fraoula*

street ο δρόμος *o dhromos*

street plan ο οδικός χάρτης *o odheekos khartees*

string ο σπάγγος *o spangos*

striped ριγωτός *reeghotos*

strong δυνατός *dheenatos*

stuck *(jammed)* κολλημένος *koleemenos*

student ο φοιτητής / η φοιτήτρια *o feeteetees / ee feeteetreea*

stung: I've been stung by something κάτι με τσίμπησε *katee me tseembeese*

stupid ανόητος *anoeetos*

suddenly ξαφνικά *ksafneeka*

suede το καστόρι *to kastoree*

sugar η ζάχαρη *ee zakharee*

suit *(man's)* το κοστούμι *to kostoomee*
  (woman's) το ταγιέρ *to tayer*

suitcase η βαλίτσα *ee valeetsa*

summer το καλοκαίρι *to kalokeree*

sun ο ήλιος *o eeleeos*

to sunbathe κάνω ηλιοθεραπεία *kano eeleeotherapeea*

sun block το αντιηλιακό *to andee-eelyako*

sunburn *(painful)* το κάψιμο από τον ήλιο *to kapseemo apo ton eeleeo*

sunglasses τα γυαλιά του ήλιου *ta yalya too eeleeoo*

sunny *(weather)* ηλιόλουστος *eelyoloostos*
sunrise η ανατολή *ee anatolee*
sunset η δύση *ee dheesee*
sunshade η ομπρέλα *ee ombrela*
sunstroke η ηλίαση *ee eeleeasee*
suntan lotion το λάδι για τον ήλιο *to ladhee ya ton eeleeo*
supermarket το σούπερμάρκετ *to supermarket*
supper το δείπνο *to dheepno*
supplement το συμπλήρωμα *to seembleeroma*
surcharge η επιβάρυνση *ee epeevareensee*
surfboard η σανίδα σέρφινγκ *ee saneedha surfing*
surfing το σέρφινγκ *to surfing*
surname το επώνυμο *to eponeemo*
surrounded by τριγυρισμένος από *treeyeereesmenos apo*
suspension η ανάρτηση *ee anarteesee*
to sweat ιδρώνω *eedhrono*
sweater το πουλόβερ *to poolover*
sweet *adj (taste)* γλυκός *ghleekos*
sweet *n* το γλυκό *to ghleeko*
sweets οι καραμέλες *ee karameles*
sweetener η ζαχαρίνη *ee zakhareenee*

to swim κολυμπώ *koleembo*
swimming pool η πισίνα *ee peeseena*
swimsuit το μαγιό *to mayo*
swing *(for children)* η κούνια *ee koonya*
switch ο διακόπτης *o dheeakoptees*
to switch on ανάβω *anavo*
to switch off σβήνω *sveeno*
swollen *(ankle, etc.)* πρησμένος *preesmenos*
synagogue η συναγωγή *ee seenaghoyee*

T

table το τραπέζι *to trapezee*
tablecloth το τραπεζομάντηλο *to trapezomandeelo*
tablespoon το κουτάλι *to kootalee*
tablet το χάπι *to khapee*
table tennis το πινγκ πονγκ *to ping pong*
to take παίρνω *perno*
to take out βγάζω *vghazo*
  (from bank account) αποσύρω *aposeero*
to talk μιλώ *meelo*
tall ψηλός *pseelos*
tame *(animal)* ήμερος *eemeros*

tampons τα ταμπόν *ta tambon*

tap η βρύση *ee vreesee*

tape recorder το μαγνητόφωνο *to maghneetofono*

to taste δοκιμάζω *dhokeemazo*

taste *n* η γεύση *ee yefsee*

tax ο φόρος *o foros*

taxi το ταξί *to taksee*

taxi rank η πιάτσα *ee pyatsa*

tea το τσάι *to tsaee*

tea bag το φακελλάκι τσαγιού *to fakelakee tsayoo*

to teach διδάσκω *dheedhasko*

teacher ο δάσκαλος / η δασκάλα *o dhaskalos / ee dhaskala*

teapot η τσαγιέρα *ee tsayera*

tear *(in eye)* το δάκρυ *to dhakree*
  (in material) το σχίσιμο *to skheeseemo*

teaspoon το κουταλάκι *to kootalakee*

teat η ρώγα *ee rogha*

teeth τα δόντια *ta dhondeea*

telegram το τηλεγράφημα *to teeleghrafeema*

telephone το τηλέφωνο *to teelefono*

telephone box ο τηλεφωνικός θάλαμος *o teelefoneekos thalamos*

telephone call το τηλεφώνημα *to teelefoneema*

telephone directory ο τηλεφωνικός κατάλογος *o teelefoneekos kataloghos*

television η τηλεόραση *ee teeleorasee*

telex το τέλεξ *to telex*

to tell λέγω *legho*
  (story) διηγούμαι *dhee-eeghoome*

temperature η θερμοκρασία *ee thermokraseea*
  to have a temperature έχω πυρετό *ekho peereto*

temple ο ναός *o naos*

temporary προσωρινός *prosoreenos*

tennis το τένις *to tenees*

tennis ball η μπάλα του τένις *ee bala too tennis*

tennis court το γήπεδο του τένις *to yeepedho too tenees*

tennis racket η ρακέτα του τένις *ee raketa too tenees*

tent η σκηνή *ee skeenee*

tent peg ο πάσσαλος της σκηνής *o pasalos tees skeenees*

terminus το τέρμα *to terma*

terrace η ταράτσα *ee taratsa*

thank you ευχαριστώ *efkhareesto*

that εκείνος *ekeenos*
  that book εκείνο το βιβλίο *ekeeno to veevleeo*
  that one εκείνο *ekeeno*

t

theatre το θέατρο *to theatro*
then τότε *tote*
there εκεί *ekee*
   there is υπάρχει *eeparkhee*
   there are υπάρχουν *eeparkhoon*
thermometer το θερμόμετρο *to thermometro*
these αυτοί / αυτές / αυτά *aftee* (masculine) / *aftes* (feminine) / *afta* (neuter)
   these books αυτά τα βιβλία *afta ta veevleea*
they αυτοί *aftee* see **GRAMMAR**
thick χοντρός *khontros*
thief ο κλέφτης *o kleftees*
thin λεπτός *leptos*
thing το πράγμα *to praghma*
third τρίτος *treetos*
thirsty: *I'm thirsty* διψάω *dheepsao*
this αυτός / αυτή / αυτό *aftos* (masculine) / *aftee* (feminine) / *afto* (neuter)
   this book αυτό το βιβλίο *afto to veevleeo*
   this one αυτό *afto*
those εκείνοι *ekeenee*
   those books εκείνα τα βιβλία *ekeena ta veevleea*
thread η κλωστή *ee klostee*

t

throat ο λαιμός *o lemos*
throat lozenges οι παστίλιες για το λαιμό *ee pasteelyes ya to lemo*
through διαμέσου *dheeamesoo*
thunder η βροντή *ee vrondee*
thunderstorm η θύελλα *ee theeela*
ticket το εισιτήριο *to eeseeteereeo*
ticket collector ο ελεγκτής *o elengtees*
ticket office η θυρίδα *ee theereedha*
tie η γραβάτα *ee ghravata*
tight σφιχτός *sfeekhtos*
tights το καλσόν *to kalson*
till *(cash)* το ταμείο *to tameeo*
till *(until)* μέχρι *mekhree*
time *(by the clock)* η ώρα *ee ora*
   what time is it? τι ώρα είναι; *tee ora eene*
timetable τα δρομολόγια *ta dhromoloya*
tin η κονσέρβα *ee konserva*
tinfoil το ασημόχαρτο *to aseemokharto*
tin-opener το ανοιχτήρι για κονσέρβες *to aneekhteeree ya konserves*

t

tip *(to waiter, etc.)* το πουρμπουάρ *to poorbooar*
tipped *(cigarettes)* με φίλτρο *me feeltro*
tired κουρασμένος *koorasmenos*
tissue το χαρτομάντηλο *to khartomandeelo*

136

to σε (στο / στη / στο) se (sto [masculine] /stee [feminine] /sto [neuter])
  to Greece στην Ελλάδα steen eladha
toast η φρυγανιά ee freeghany**a**
tobacco ο καπνός o kapn**o**s
tobacconists το καπνοπωλείο to kapnopol**ee**o
today σήμερα s**ee**mera
together μαζί maz**ee**
toilet η τουαλέτα ee tooal**e**ta
toilet paper το χαρτί υγείας to khart**ee** eey**ee**as
toll τα διόδια ta dhee**o**dheea
tomato η ντομάτα ee dom**a**ta
tomato juice ο χυμός ντομάτας o kheem**o**s dom**a**tas
tomorrow αύριο **a**vreeo
tongue η γλώσσα ee ghl**o**sa
tonic water το τόνικ to t**o**neek
tonight απόψε ap**o**pse
too (also) επίσης ep**ee**sees
  (too much) πάρα πολύ p**a**ra pol**ee**
tooth το δόντι to dh**o**ndee
toothache ο πονόδοντος o pon**o**dhondos
toothbrush η οδοντόβουρτσα ee odhont**o**voortsa
toothpaste η οδοντόκρεμα ee odhond**o**krema
top το πάνω μέρος to p**a**no m**e**ros
  (of mountain) η κορυφή ee koreef**ee**
torch ο φακός o fak**o**s
torn σχισμένος skheesm**e**nos
total το σύνολο to s**ee**nolo
tough (of meat) σκληρός skleer**o**s
tour η περιοδεία ee pereeodh**ee**a
tourist ο τουρίστας / η τουρίστρια o toor**ee**stas / ee toor**ee**streea
tourist office το τουριστικό γραφείο to tooreesteek**o** ghraf**ee**o
tourist ticket το τουριστικό εισιτήριο to tooreesteek**o** eeseetee**r**eeo
to tow ρυμουλκώ reemoolk**o**
towel η πετσέτα ee pets**e**ta
tower ο πύργος o p**ee**rghos
town η πόλη ee p**o**lee
town centre το κέντρο της πόλης to k**e**ndro tees p**o**lees
town hall το δημαρχείο to dheemarkh**ee**o
town plan ο χάρτης της πόλης o kh**a**rtees tees p**o**lees
towrope το σχοινί ρυμούλκησης to skheen**ee** reem**oo**lkeesees
toy το παιγνίδι to peghn**ee**dhee
traditional παραδοσιακός paradhosyak**o**s
traffic η κυκλοφορία ee keeklofor**ee**a
traffic lights τα φανάρια της τροχαίας ta fan**a**reea tees trokh**e**as

t

trailer το τρέιλερ *to trailer*
train το τρένο *to treno*
training shoes τα αθλητικά παπούτσια *ta athleeteeka papootsya*
tram το τραμ *to tram*
to translate μεταφράζω *metafrazo*
translation η μετάφραση *ee metafrasee*
to travel ταξιδεύω *takseedhevo*
travel agent ο ταξιδιωτικός πράκτορας *o takseedhyoteekos praktoras*
travellers' cheques τα ταξιδιωτικά τσεκ *ta takseedhyoteeka tsek*
tray ο δίσκος *o dheeskos*
tree το δέντρο *to dhendro*
trim *n (hair)* το κόψιμο *to kopseemo*
trip η εκδρομή *ee ekdhromee*
trolley bus το τρόλεϋ *to troley*
trouble ο μπελάς *o belas*
trousers το παντελόνι *to pandelonee*
trout η πέστροφα *ee pestrofa*
true αληθινός *aleetheenos*
trunk το μπαούλο *to baoolo*
trunks το μαγιό *to mayo*
to try προσπαθώ *prospatho*
to try on δοκιμάζω *dhokeemazo*
T-shirt το μπλουζάκι *to bloozakee*
tuna ο τόνος *o tonos*
tunnel η σήραγγα *ee seeranga*
turkey η γαλοπούλα *ee ghalopoola*
to turn γυρίζω *yeereezo*
turnip η ρέβα *ee reva*
to turn off *(on a journey)* στρίβω *streevo*
  (radio, etc.) κλείνω *kleeno*
  (engine, light) σβήνω *sveeno*
to turn on *(radio, etc.)* ανοίγω *aneegho*
  (engine, light) ανάβω *anavo*
TV η τηλεόραση *ee teeleorasee*
tweezers το τσιμπίδι *to tseembeedhee*
twice δύο φορές *dheeo fores*
twin ο δίδυμος *o dheedheemos*
twin-bedded το δίκλινο δωμάτιο *to dheekleeno dhomateeo*
to type δακτυλογραφώ *dhakteeloghrafo*
typical τυπικός *teepeekos*
tyre το λάστιχο *to lasteekho*
tyre pressure η πίεση στα λάστιχα *ee peeyesee sta lasteekha*

138

U

ugly άσχημος *askheemos*
umbrella η ομπρέλα *ee ombrela*
uncle ο θείος *o theeos*
uncomfortable άβολος *avolos*
unconscious αναίσθητος *anestheetos*
under κάτω από *kato apo*
underground *(railway)* το μετρό *to metro*
underpants *(men's)* το σώβρακο *to sovrako*
underpass η υπόγεια διάβαση *ee eepoyeea dheeavasee*
to understand καταλαβαίνω *katalaveno*
underwear τα εσώρουχα *ta esorookha*
unemployed άνεργος *anerghos*
unfasten λύνω *leeno*
United States οι Ηνωμένες Πολιτείες *ee eenomenes poleeteeyes*
university το πανεπιστήμιο *to panepeesteemeeo*
unleaded petrol η αμόλυβδη βενζίνη *ee amoleevdhee venzeenee*
to unpack *(case)* αδειάζω *adheeazo*
up *(out of bed)* ξύπνιος *kseepneeos*
  to go up ανεβαίνω *aneveno*
upstairs πάνω *pano*
urgently επειγόντως *epeeghondos*
urine τα ούρα *ta oora*
urn ο αμφορέας *o amforeas*
to use χρησιμοποιώ *khreeseemopyo*
useful χρήσιμος *khreeseemos*
usual συνηθισμένος *seeneetheesmenos*
usually συνήθως *seeneethos*

V

vacancy *(room)* το διαθέσιμο δωμάτιο *to dheeatheseemo dhomateeo*
vacuum cleaner η ηλεκτρική σκούπα *ee eelektreekee skoopa*
valid έγκυρος *engeeros*
valley η κοιλάδα *ee keeladha*
valuable πολύτιμος *poleeteemos*
valuables τα πολύτιμα αντικείμενα *ta poleeteema andeekeemena*
value η αξία *ee akseea*
van το φορτηγάκι *to forteeghakee*
vase το βάζο *to vazo*
VAT ο ΦΠΑ *o fee pee a*
veal το μοσχάρι *to moskharee*
vegetables τα λαχανικά *ta lakhaneeka*

v   **vegetarian** ο χορτοφάγος *o khortofaghos*
vein η φλέβα *ee fleva*
velvet το βελούδο *to veloodho*
ventilator ο εξαεριστήρας *o eksaereesteeras*
very πολύ *polee*
vest η φανέλα *ee fanela*
via μέσω *meso*
video το βίντεο *to veedeo*
video camera η βιντεοκάμερα *ee veedeokamera*
video recorder η συσκευή βίντεο *ee seeskevee veedeo*
view η θέα *ee thea*
villa η βίλλα *ee veela*
village το χωριό *to khoryo*
vine leaves τα κληματόφυλλα *ta kleematofeela*
vinegar το ξύδι *to kseedhee*
visa η βίζα *ee veesa*
to visit επισκέπτομαι *epeeskeptome*
visit επίσκεψη *ee epeeskepsee*
vitamin η βιταμίνη *ee veetameenee*
vodka η βότκα *ee votka*
voice η φωνή *ee fonee*
v   **volleyball** το βόλεϊμπολ *to volleyball*
voltage η τάση *ee tasee*

W

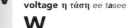

wage ο μισθός *o meesthos*
waist η μέση *ee mesee*
to wait for περιμένω *pereemeno*
waiter το γκαρσόνι *to garsonee*
waiting room η αίθουσα αναμονής *ee ethoosa anamonees*
waitress η σερβιτόρα *ee serveetora*
Wales η Ουαλία *ee ooaleea*
walk ο περίπατος *o pereepatos*
to walk περπατώ *perpato*
walking stick το μπαστούνι *to bastoonee*
wall ο τοίχος *o teekhos*
wallet το πορτοφόλι *to portofolee*
walnut το καρύδι *to kareedhee*
to want θέλω *thelo*
w   **war** ο πόλεμος *o polemos*
wardrobe η γκαρνταρόμπα *ee gardaroba*
warm ζεστός *zestos*
warning triangle το τρίγωνο αυτοκινήτου *to treeghono aftokeeneetoo*

140

to wash *(clothes)* πλένω *pleno*
  (oneself) πλένομαι *plenome*
washbasin η νιπτήρας *ee neepteeras*
washing machine το πλυντήριο *to pleendeereeo*
washing powder το απορρυπαντικό *to aporeepandeeko*
washing-up liquid το υγρό για τα πιάτα *to eeghro ya ta pyata*
wasp η σφήκα *ee sfeeka*
waste bin το καλάθι των αχρήστων *to kalathee ton akhreeston*
watch *n* το ρολόι *to roloee*
to watch *(TV)* βλέπω *vlepo*
  (someone's luggage) προσέχω *prosekho*
watchstrap το λουρί του ρολογιού *to looree too rologhyoo*
water το νερό *to nero*
  fresh water το γλυκό νερό *to ghleeko nero*
  salt water το αλμυρό νερό *to almeero nero*
waterfall ο καταρράκτης *o kataraktees*
water heater ο θερμοσίφωνας *o thermoseefonas*
water-skiing το θαλάσσιο σκι *to thalaseeo skee*
watermelon το καρπούζι *to karpoozee*
waterproof αδιάβροχος *adheeavrokhos*
wave *(on sea)* το κύμα *to keema*
wax το κερί *to keree*
way *(method)* ο τρόπος *o tropos*
  this way από 'δω *apodho*
  that way από 'κει *apokee*
we εμείς *emees*
weak αδύνατος *adheenatos*
to wear φορώ *foro*
weather ο καιρός *o keros*
wedding ο γάμος *o ghamos*
week η εβδομάδα *ee evdhomadha*
weekday η καθημερινή *ee katheemereenee*
weekend το σαββατοκύριακο *to savatokeereeako*
weekly *(rate, etc.)* εβδομαδιαίος *evdhomadhyeos*
weight το βάρος *to varos*
welcome καλώς ήλθατε *kalos eelthate*
well *(healthy)* υγιής *eeyee-ees*
well done *(steak)* καλοψημένος *kalopseemenos*
Welsh *(person)* ο Ουαλός / η Ουαλή *o ooalos / ee ooalee*
west η δύση *ee dheesee*
wet *(damp)* βρεγμένος *vreghmenos*
  (weather) βροχερός *vrokheros*
wetsuit η στολή για υποβρύχιο ψάρεμα *ee stolee ya eepovreekheeo psarema*
what τι *tee*

141

what is it? τι είναι; *tee eene*

wheel ο τροχός *o trokhos*

wheelchair η αναπηρική καρέκλα *ee anapeereekee karekla*

when? πότε; *pote*

where? πού; *poo*

which? ποιος; *pyos*
  which is it? ποιο είναι; *pyo eene*

while ενώ *eno*

whipped cream η σαντιγί *ee sandeeyee*

whisky το ουίσκυ *to whisky*

white άσπρος *aspros*

who ποιος *pyos*

whole όλος *olos*

wholemeal bread ψωμί ολικής αλέσεως *psomee oleekees aleseos*

whose: whose is it? ποιου είναι; *pyoo eene*

why? γιατί; *yatee*

wide πλατύς *platees*

wife η σύζυγος *ee seezeeghos*

wind ο αέρας *o aeras*

window το παράθυρο *to paratheero*

windmill ο ανεμόμυλος *o anemomeelo*

windscreen το παρμπρίζ *to parbreez*

windsurfing το γουιντσέρφινγκ *to windsurfing*

wine το κρασί *to krasee*

wine list ο κατάλογος των κρασιών *o kataloghos ton krasyon*

wine shop η κάβα *ee kava*

winter ο χειμώνας *o kheemonas*

with με *me*

without χωρίς *khorees*

woman η γυναίκα *ee yeeneka*

wood το ξύλο *to kseelo*

wool το μαλλί *to malee*

word η λέξη *ee leksee*

to work (person) δουλεύω *dhoolevo*
  (machine) λειτουργεί *leetooryee*

worried ανήσυχος *aneeseekhos*

worse χειρότερος *kheeroteros*

worth: 2000 drachmas worth of petrol 2000 δραχμές βενζίνη *dheeo kheelyadhes dhrakhmes venzeenee*
  it's worth 2000 drachmas αξίζει 2000 δραχμές *akseezee dheeo kheelyadhes dhrakhmes*

to wrap (up) τυλίγω *teeleegho*

wrapping paper το χαρτί περιτυλίγματος *to khartee pereeteeleeghmatos*

to write γράφω *ghrafo*

writing paper το χαρτί αλληλογραφίας *to khartee aleeloghrafeeas*
wrong λάθος *lathos*
  you're wrong κάνετε λάθος *kanete lathos*

Y

yacht το γιοτ *to yacht*
year ο χρόνος *o khronos*
yellow κίτρινος *keetreenos*
yes ναι *ne*
yesterday χτες *khtes*
yet ακόμα *akoma*
  not yet όχι ακόμα *okhee akoma*
yoghurt το γιαούρτι *to yaoortee*
you *(singular/plural)* εσύ **/** εσείς *esee / esees*
young νέος *neos*
youth hostel ο ξενώνας νεότητος *o ksenonas neoteetos*

Z

zero το μηδέν *to meedhen*
zip το φερμουάρ *to fermooar*
zone η ζώνη *ee zonee*
zoo ο ζωολογικός κήπος *o zooloyeekos keepos*

αβγό (το) egg
  αβγά ημέρας newly-laid eggs
άγαλμα (το) statue
αγάπη (η) love
αγαπώ to love
αγγείο (το) vessel ; urn
αγγειοπλαστική (η) pottery *(craft)*
αγγελία (η) announcement
άγγελος (ο) angel
Αγγλία (η) England
αγγλικός/ή/ό English *(thing)*
Άγγλος/Αγγλίδα (ο/η) Englishman/-woman
αγγούρι (το) cucumber
άγιος/α/ο holy ; saint
  Άγιον Όρος (το) Mount Athos
αγκινάρα (η) artichoke
άγκυρα (η) anchor
αγορά (η) agora ; market
αγοράζω to buy
αγοραστής (ο) buyer
αγόρι (το) young boy
άδεια (η) permit ; licence
  άδεια οδηγήσεως driving licence
άδειος/α/ο empty
αδελφή (η) sister
αδελφός (ο) brother
αδιάβροχο (το) raincoat
αδιέξοδο (το) cul-de-sac ; no through road
αδίκημα (το) offence
αέρας (ο) wind
αερογραμμές (οι) airways
  Βρετανικές Αερογραμμές British Airways
  Κυπριακές Αερογραμμές Cyprus Airways
αεροδρόμιο (το) airport
αερολιμένας/αερολιμήν(ο) airport
αεροπλάνο (το) aeroplane
αεροπορία (η) air force
  Ολυμπιακή Αεροπορία Olympic Airways
αεροπορικό εισιτήριο (το) air ticket
αεροπορικώς by air
αζήτητος/η/ο unclaimed
Αθήνα (η) Athens

α A	**α**
β B	
γ Γ	
δ Δ	
ε E	
ζ Z	
η H	
θ Θ	
ι I	
κ K	
λ Λ	
μ M	
ν N	**α**
ξ Ξ	
ο O	
π Π	
ρ P	
σ ς Σ	
τ T	
υ Y	
φ Φ	
χ X	
ψ Ψ	**α**
ω Ω	

α A	αθλητικό κέντρο (το) sports centre
	αθλητισμός (ο) sports
β B	Αιγαίο (το) the Aegean Sea
γ Γ	αίθουσα (η) room
	αίθουσα αναμονής waiting room
δ Δ	αίθουσα αναχωρήσεων departure lounge
	αιμορραγώ to bleed
ε E	αίμα (το) to bleed
ζ Z	αίτημα (το) demand
	αίτηση (η) application
η H	ακάθαρτος/η/ο dirty
	ακουστικά (τα) earphones
θ Θ	ακουστικά βαρυκοΐας hearing aids
	ακουστικό (το) receiver *(telephone)*
ι I	ακούω to hear
	άκρη (η) edge
κ K	Ακρόπολη/ις (η) the Acropolis
	ακτή (η) beach ; shore
λ Λ	ακτινογραφία (η) X-ray
	ακυρώνω to cancel
μ M	αλάτι (το) salt
ν N	αλεύρι (το) flour
	αλιεία (η) fishing
ξ Ξ	είδη αλιείας fishing tackle
	αλλαγή (η) change
ο O	αλλάζω to change
	δεν αλλάζονται goods will not be exchanged
π Π	αλληλογραφία (η) correspondence
ρ P	αλληλογραφώ to correspond
	αλλοδαπός/ή foreign national
σ ς Σ	αστυνομία αλλοδαπών immigration police
	αλμυρός/ή/ό salty
τ T	αλτ! stop!
υ Y	αλυσίδα (η) chain
	αμάξωμα (το) body *(of car)*
φ Φ	αμερικάνικος/η/ο American *(thing)*
χ X	Αμερικανός/Αμερικανίδα American *(man/woman)*
	Αμερική (η) America
ψ Ψ	αμέσως at once ; immediately
	αμήν amen
ω Ω	άμμος (η) sand
	αμμουδιά (η) sandy beach

αμοιβή (η) reward ; fare ; salary ; payment
αμπέλι (το) vine
αμύγδαλο (το) almond
αμφιθέατρο (το) amphitheatre
αμφορέας (ο) jar ; amphor
αν if
αναβολή (η) delay
ανάβω to switch on
αναγγελία (η) announcement
αναζήτηση (η) search
ανάκριση (η) interrogation
ανάκτορα (τα) palace
αναμονή (η) waiting
  αίθουσα αναμονής waiting room
ανανάς (ο) pineapple
ανανεώνω to renew
ανάπηρος/η/ο handicapped ; disabled
αναπληρώνω to replace
αναπτήρας (ο) cigarette lighter
ανασκαφή (η) excavation
ανατολή (η) east ; sunrise
ανατολικός/ή/ό eastern

ΑΝΑΧΩΡΗΣΕΙΣ DEPARTURES

αναψυκτήριο (το) refreshment
αναψυκτικό (το) soft drink
αναψυχή (η) recreation ; pleasure
άνδρας (ο) man

ΑΝΔΡΕΣ GENTS

ανδρική μόδα (η) mens fashions
ανελκυστήρας (ο) lift ; elevator
ανεμιστήρας (ο) fan
άνθη (τα) flowers
ανθοπωλείο (το) florist's
άνθρωπος (ο) man
ανοίγω to open

ΑΝΟΙΚΤΟ OPEN

άνοιξη (η) spring
ανταλλαγή (η) exchange

α A
β B
γ Γ
δ Δ
ε E
ζ Z
η H
θ Θ
ι I
κ K
λ Λ
μ M
ν N
ξ Ξ
ο O
π Π
ρ P
σ ς Σ
τ T
υ Y
φ Φ
χ X
ψ Ψ
ω Ω

α

α

α

147

α Α	ανταλλακτικά (τα) spare parts
β Β	αντιβιοτικά (τα) antibiotics
	αντίγραφο (το) copy ; reproduction
γ Γ	αντίκες (οι) antiques
δ Δ	αντικλεπτικά (τα) anti-theft devices
	αντίο goodbye
ε Ε	αντιπηκτικό (το) antifreeze
ζ Ζ	αντιπρόσωπος (ο) representative
	αντλία (η) pump
η Η	αντλία βενζίνης petrol pump
	αντρόγυνο (το) couple
θ Θ	ανώμαλος/η/ο uneven ; rough
	αξεσουάρ (τα) accessories
ι Ι	αξεσουάρ αυτοκινήτου car accessories
κ Κ	αξία (η) value
	αξία διαδρομής fare
λ Λ	αξιοθέατα (τα) the sights
	απαγορεύω to forbid ; no...
μ Μ	απαγορεύεται η αναμονή no waiting
	απαγορεύεται η διάβαση keep off
ν Ν	απαγορεύεται η είσοδος no entry
	απαγορεύεται το κάπνισμα no smoking
ξ Ξ	απαγορεύεται η στάθμευση no parking
	απαγορεύονται τα σκυλιά no dogs
ο Ο	απαγορεύεται η φωτογράφηση no photography
	απαγορεύεται το κολύμπι no swimming
π Π	απαγορεύεται η κατασκήνωση no camping
	απαίτηση (η) claim
ρ Ρ	απεργία (η) strike
	απογείωση (η) takeoff
σ ς Σ	απόγευμα (το) afternoon
	απόδειξη (η) receipt
τ Τ	αποθήκη (η) warehouse
	αποκλειστικός/ή/ό exclusive
υ Υ	απόκριες (οι) carnival
	αποσκευές (οι) luggage
φ Φ	αναζήτηση αποσκευών left-luggage *(office)*
	απόχη (η) fishing/butterfly net
χ Χ	απόψε tonight
ψ Ψ	ΑΠΡΙΛΙΟΣ APRIL
	αργότερα later
ω Ω	αρέσω to please

μου αρέσει I like
  δεν μου αρέσει I don't like
αριθμός (ο) number
  αριθμός διαβατηρίου passport number
  αριθμός πτήσεως flight number
  αριθμός τηλεφώνου telephone number
αριστερά left *(side)*
αρνί (το) lamb
αρρώστια (η) illness
άρρωστος/η/ο ill
  άρρωστος/η (ο/η) patient
αρτοποιία (η) bakery
αρχαιολογικός χώρος (ο) archaeological site
αρχαίος/α/ο ancient
αρχή (η) start ; authority
αρχίζω to begin ; to start
άρωμα (το) perfume
ασανσέρ (το) lift ; elevator
ασθενής (ο/η) patient
άσθμα (το) asthma
άσκοπος/η/ο improper
  άσκοπη χρήση improper use
ασπιρίνη (η) aspirin
άσπρος/η/ο white
αστακός (ο) lobster
αστικός νομισματοδέκτης (ο) coin-operated phone for
  local calls
αστυνομία (η) police
  αστυνομία αλλοδαπών immigration police
  Ελληνική αστυνομία Greek police
αστυνομική διάταξη (η) police notice
αστυνομική τμήμα (η) police station
αστυνομικός σταθμός (ο) police station
αστυνόμος (ο) policeman
αστυφύλακας (ο) town policeman
ασφάλεια (η) insurance ; fuse
  ασφάλεια έναντι κλοπής theft insurance
  ασφάλεια έναντι τρίτων third-party insurance
  ασφάλεια ζωής life insurance
ασφάλιση (η) insurance
  πλήρης ασφάλιση comprehensive insurance
  ιατρική ασφάλιση medical insurance
ατμοπλοϊκό εισιτήριο (το) boat ticket

α A	**α**
β B	
γ Γ	
δ Δ	
ε Ε	
ζ Ζ	
η Η	
θ Θ	
ι Ι	
κ Κ	
λ Λ	
μ Μ	
ν Ν	**α**
ξ Ξ	
ο Ο	
π Π	
ρ Ρ	
σ ς Σ	
τ Τ	
υ Υ	
φ Φ	
χ Χ	
ψ Ψ	**α**
ω Ω	

α Α	
β Β	
γ Γ	
δ Δ	
ε Ε	
ζ Ζ	
η Η	
θ Θ	
ι Ι	
κ Κ	
λ Λ	
μ Μ	
ν Ν	
ξ Ξ	
ο Ο	
π Π	
ρ Ρ	
σ ς Σ	
τ Τ	
υ Υ	
φ Φ	
χ Χ	
ψ Ψ	
ω Ω	

ατομικός/ή/ό personal
άτομο (το) person
  άτομο τρίτης ηλικίας pensioner
ατύχημα (το) accident
αυγό (το) egg

ΑΥΓΟΥΣΤΟΣ AUGUST

αυτοκίνητο (το) car
  ενοικιάσεις αυτοκινήτων car hire
  συνεργείο αυτοκινήτων car repairs
αυτοκινητόδρομος (ο) motorway
αυτόματος/η/ο automatic
άφιξη (η) arrival

ΑΦΙΞΕΙΣ ARRIVALS

αφορολόγητα (τα) duty-free goods
Αφροδίτη Aphrodite ; Venus
αχλάδι (το) pear
άχρηστα (τα) waste
αψίδα (η) arch

β Β

βαγόνι (το) carriage (train)
βαλβίδα (η) valve
βαλίτσα (η) suitcase
βαμβακερός/ή/ό (made of) cotton
βαρέλι (το) barrel
  μπίρα από βαρέλι draught beer
  βαρελίσιο κρασί (το) house wine
βάρκα (η) boat
βάρος (το) weight
βαφή (η) paint ; dye
βάφω to paint
βγάζω to take off
βγαίνω to go out
βελόνα (η) needle
βενζίνη (η) petrol ; gasoline
βήχας (ο) cough
βιβλίο (το) book
βιβλιοθήκη (η) bookcase ; library
  Δημοτική Βιβλιοθήκη Public Library
  Κεντρική Βιβλιοθήκη Central Library

βιβλιοπωλείο (το) bookshop
Βίβλος (η) the Bible
βιταμίνη (η) vitamin
βιτρίνα (η) shop window
βοδινό κρέας beef
βοήθεια (η) help
  οδική βοήθεια breakdown service
  πρώτες βοήθειες casualty (hospital)
βόμβα (η) bomb
βομβητής (ο) buzzer ; bleeper
βόρειος/α/ο northern
βορράς (ο) north
βουλή (η) parliament
βουνό (το) mountain
βούρτσα (η) brush
βούτυρο (το) butter
βράδυ (το) evening
βράζω to cook
βραστός/ή/ό cooked
Βρετανία (η) Britain
βρετανικός/ή/ό British (thing)
Βρετανός/Βρετανίδα (ο/η) British (man/woman)
βροχή (η) rain

γ Γ

γάιδαρος (ο) donkey
γάλα (το) milk
γαλάζιος/α/ο blue ; light blue
γαλακτοπωλείο (το) dairy shop
Γαλλία (η) France
γαλλικός/ή/ό French (thing)
Γάλλος/Γαλλίδα (ο/η) French (man/woman)
γαλοπούλα (η) turkey
γάμος (ο) wedding ; marriage
γαμήλια δεξίωση wedding reception
γαρίδα (η) shrimp ; prawn
γειά σας hello ; goodbye (formal)
γειά σου hello ; goodbye (informal)
γεμάτος/η/ο full
γενέθλια (τα) birthday
γενικός/ή/ό general

| α A |
| β B |
| γ Γ |
| δ Δ |
| ε E |
| ζ Z |
| η H |
| θ Θ |
| ι I |
| κ K |
| λ Λ |
| μ M |
| ν N |
| ξ Ξ |
| o O |
| π Π |
| ρ P |
| σ ς Σ |
| τ T |
| υ Y |
| φ Φ |
| χ X |
| ψ Ψ |
| ω Ω |

α Α	
β Β	
γ Γ	
δ Δ	
ε Ε	
ζ Ζ	
η Η	
θ Θ	
ι Ι	
κ Κ	
λ Λ	
μ Μ	
ν Ν	
ξ Ξ	
ο Ο	
π Π	
ρ Ρ	
σ ς Σ	
τ Τ	
υ Υ	
φ Φ	
χ Χ	
ψ Ψ	
ω Ω	

Γενικό Νοσοκομείο General Hospital
γέννηση (η) birth
Γερμανία (η) Germany
γερμανικός/ή/ό German (thing)
Γερμανός/Γερμανίδα (ο/η) German (man/woman)
γεμιστός/ή/ό stuffed
γεύμα (το) meal
γέφυρα (η) bridge
για for
γιαγιά (η) grandmother
γιαούρτι (το) yoghurt
γιασεμί (το) jasmine
γιατί; why?
γιατρός (ο/η) doctor
γίνομαι to become
   γίνονται δεκτές πιστωτικές κάρτες we accept credit
   cards
γιορτή (η) feast ; celebration ; name day
γιος (ο) son
γιοτ (το) yacht
γκάζι (το) accelerator (car) ; gas
γκαλερί art gallery ; art sales
γκαράζ (το) garage
γκαρσόν (το)/γκαρσόνι (το) waiter
γλυκός/ιά/ό sweet
   γλυκό (το)/γλυκά (τα) cakes and pastries ; desserts
   γλυκό ταψιού traditional pastries with syrup
γλύπτης/γλύπτρια (ο/η) sculptor
γλυπτική (η) sculpture
γλώσσα (η) tongue ; language ; sole (fish)
γονείς (οι) parents
γουιντσέρφινγκ (το) windsurfing
γράμμα (το) letter
   γράμμα κατεπείγον express letter
   γράμμα συστημένο registered letter
γραμμάριο (το) gramme
γραμματοκιβώτιο (το) letter box
γραμματόσημο (το) stamp
γραφείο (το) office ; desk
   Γραφείο Τουρισμού Tourist Office
γρήγορα quickly
γρίππη (η) influenza

γυαλί (το) glass
  γυαλιά (τα) glasses
  γυαλιά ηλίου sunglasses
γυαλικός/ή/ό made of glass
γυναίκα (η) woman

ΓΥΝΑΙΚΩΝ LADIES

γύρω round ; about
γωνία (η) corner

δ Δ

δακτυλίδι (το) ring (for finger)
δακτύλιος (ο) ring ; circle
δαμάσκηνο (το) plum
δαντέλα (η) lace
δασκάλα (η) teacher (female)
δάσκαλος (ο) teacher (male)
δασμός (ο) duty ; tax
δάσος (το) forest
δείπνο (το) dinner
δέκα ten

ΔΕΚΕΜΒΡΙΟΣ DECEMBER

δελτίο (το) card ; coupon
  δελτίο αφίξεως arrival card
δελφίνι (το) dolphin
  ιπτάμενο δελφίνι hydrofoil
Δελφοί (οι) Delphi
δέμα (το) parcel
Δεμέστιχα dry wine (white or red)
δεν not
  δεν δίνει ρέστα no change given

ΔΕ ΛΕΙΤΟΥΡΓΕΙ OUT OF ORDER

δεξιά right (side)
δέρμα (το) skin ; leather
δεσποινίς/δεσποινίδα (η) Miss

ΔΕΥΤΕΡΑ MONDAY

δεύτερος/η/ο second
δήλωση (η) announcement
  δήλωση συναλλάγματος currency declaration
  είδη προς δήλωση goods to declare

α A	γ
β B	
γ Γ	
δ Δ	
ε E	
ζ Z	
η H	
θ Θ	
ι I	
κ K	
λ Λ	
μ M	
ν N	δ
ξ Ξ	
ο O	
π Π	
ρ P	
σ ς Σ	
τ T	
υ Y	
φ Φ	
χ X	
ψ Ψ	δ
ω Ω	

153

δ

α Α	ουδέν προς δήλωση nothing to declare
β Β	δημαρχείο (το) town hall
γ Γ	δημόσιος/α/ο public
	δημόσια έργα road works
δ Δ	δημόσιος κήπος public gardens
	δημοτικός/ή/ό public
ε Ε	Δημοτική Αγορά public market
ζ Ζ	Δημοτική Βιβλιοθήκη Public Library
	διάβαση (η) crossing
η Η	διάβαση πεζών pedestrian crossing
θ Θ	υπόγεια διάβαση πεζών pedestrian subway
	διαβατήριο (το) passport
ι Ι	αριθμός διαβατηρίου passport number
κ Κ	έλεγχος διαβατηρίων passport control
	διαβήτης (ο) diabetes
λ Λ	διαδρομή (η) route
μ Μ	δίαιτα (η) diet
	διακεκριμένος/η/ο distinguished
ν Ν	διακεκριμένη θέση business class
ξ Ξ	διακοπές (οι) holidays
	διάλειμμα (το) interval ; break
ο Ο	διάλυση (η) closing down (sale) ; dilution
π Π	διαμέρισμα (το) flat ; apartment
	διανυχτερεύει open all-night
ρ Ρ	διάρκεια (η) duration
	κατά τη διάρκεια της ημέρας during the day
σ ς Σ	διασκέδαση (η) entertainment
τ Τ	κέντρο διασκεδάσεως nightclub
	διατηρώ to keep ; to preserve
υ Υ	διατηρείτε την πόλη καθαρή keep the town clean
φ Φ	διατροφή (η) diet
	διεθνής/ής/ές international
χ Χ	διερμηνέας (ο/η) interpreter
ψ Ψ	διεύθυνση (η) address
	διευθυντής (ο) manager
ω Ω	δικαστήριο (το) court
	δικηγόρος (ο/η) lawyer
	διπλός/ή/ό double
	διπλό δωμάτιο double room
	διπλό κρεββάτι double bed
	δισκοθήκη (η) disco (Cyprus) ; music collection
	δίσκος (ο) record
	δίχτυ (το) net

διψώ to be thirsty
διώρυγα canal
δολάριο (το) dollar
δόντι (το) tooth
δράμα (το) drama ; play
δραχμή (η) drachma
δρομολόγιο (το) timetable ; route
  δρομολόγια εξωτερικού international routes
  δρομολόγια εσωτερικού domestic routes
δρόμος (ο) street ; way
δύση (η) west ; sunset
δυσκοιλιότητα (η) constipation
δυστύχημα (το) accident ; mishap
δυτικός/ή/ό western
Δωδεκάνησα (τα) the Dodecanese
δωμάτιο (το) room
δωρεάν free of charge
δώρο (το) present ; gift

ε E

εβδομάδα (η) week
εγγραφή (η) registration
εγγύηση (η) guarantee
έγχρωμος/η/ο coloured
  έγχρωμες φωτογραφίες colour photographs
εδώ here
EE EU
εθνικός/ή/ό national
  Εθνικό Θέατρο National Theatre
  εθνικός οδός motorway
  Εθνικός Κήπος National Garden (in Athens)
  εθνικός ύμνος national anthem
έθνος (το) nation
ειδικός/ή/ό special ; specialist
είδος (το) kind ; sort
  είδη goods
  είδη προς δήλωση goods to declare
  είδη εξοχής camping equipment
  είδη καπνιστού tobacconist
  είδη κήπου garden centre
εισιτήριο (το) ticket
  απλό εισιτήριο single ticket
  εισιτήριο με επιστροφή return ticket

α Α	ατμοπλοϊκό εισιτήριο boat ticket
	σιδηροδρομικό εισιτήριο rail ticket
β Β	φοιτητικό εισιτήριο student ticket
γ Γ	ΕΙΣΟΔΟΣ ENTRANCE
	εισπράκτορας (ο) conductor *(on bus)*
δ Δ	χωρίς εισπράκτορα pay as you enter ; prepaid
ε Ε	εκδόσεις εισιτηρίων tickets
	εκδοτήρια (τα) ticket machines
ζ Ζ	εκεί there
η Η	έκθεση (η) exhibition
	εκθεσιακό κέντρο exhibition centre
θ Θ	εκκλησία (η) church ; chapel
	έκπτωση (η) discount
ι Ι	ΕΚΠΤΩΣΕΙΣ SALE
κ Κ	εκτελούνται έργα road works
λ Λ	εκτός except ; unless
	εκτός λειτουργίας out of order
μ Μ	έλα! come on!
	ελαιόλαδο (το) olive oil
ν Ν	ελαστικό (το) tyre
	σέρβις ελαστικών tyre service
ξ Ξ	ελαττώνω to reduce ; to decrease
	ελαττώσατε ταχύτητα reduce speed
ο Ο	έλεγχος (ο) control
	έλεγχος διαβατηρίων passport control
π Π	έλεγχος εισιτηρίων check-in
	έλεγχος ελαστικών tyre check
ρ Ρ	αγορανομικός έλεγχος approved prices
σ ς Σ	ΕΛΕΥΘΕΡΟ FREE
	ελιά (η) olive ; olive tree
τ Τ	έλκος (το) ulcer
υ Υ	Ελλάδα/Ελλάς (η) Greece/Hellas
	Έλληνας/Ελληνίδα (ο/η) Greek *(man/woman)*
φ Φ	ελληνικά (τα) Greek *(language)*
	ελληνικός/ή/ό Greek *(thing)*
χ Χ	Ελληνικά Ταχυδρομεία Greek Post Office (ELTA)
	Ελληνική Δημοκρατία Republic of Greece
ψ Ψ	Ελληνικής κατασκευής Made in Greece
	το Ελληνικό Athens Airport
ω Ω	Ελληνικός Οργανισμός Τουρισμού Greek Tourist
	Organisation (EOT)

Ελληνικό προϊόν product of Greece
ΕΛΞΑΤΕ PULL

εμπρός forward ; in front
εμφανίζω to develop (film)
εμφάνιση (η) film development
εναντίον against
έναρξη (η) opening ; beginning
ένας/μία/ένα one
ένδυμα (το) article of clothing
  έτοιμα ενδύματα ready-to-wear clothing
ένεση (η) injection
ενήλικος (ο) adult
εννέα/εννιά nine
ενοικιάζω to rent ; to hire
  ενοικιάζεται to let
ενοικιάσεις for hire
ενοίκιο (το) rent
ενορία (η) parish
εντάξει all right ; OK
εντομοκτόνο (το) insecticide
έντυπο (το) form (to fill in)
έξι six

ΕΞΟΔΟΣ EXIT

εξοχή (η) countryside
εξυπηρέτηση (η) service
εξυπηρετώ to serve
έξω out ; outside
εξωλέμβιες (οι) outboard motorboats
εξώστης (ο) circle ; balcony (theatre)
εξωτερικός/ή/ό external
  το εξωτερικό abroad
  εξωτερικού letters abroad (on postbox)
  πτήσεις εξωτερικού international flights
ΕΟΚ EEC (EC)
ΕΟΤ Greek/Hellenic Tourist Organization
επάγγελμα (το) occupation ; profession
επείγον/επείγουσα urgent ; express
  επείγοντα περιστατικά casualty department
επιβάτης/τρια (ο/η) passenger
  διερχόμενοι επιβάτες passengers in transit

α A
β B
γ Γ
δ Δ
ε E
ζ Z
η H
θ Θ
ι I
κ K
λ Λ
μ M
ν N
ξ Ξ
o O
π Π
ρ P
σ ς Σ
τ T
υ Y
φ Φ
χ X
ψ Ψ
ω Ω

α A	επιβατικά (τα) private cars
β B	επιβεβαιώνω to confirm
	επιβίβαση (η) boarding
	κάρτα επιβιβάσεως boarding card
γ Γ	επιδόρπιο (το) dessert
δ Δ	επικίνδυνος/η/ο dangerous
	επίσης also
ε E	επισκεπτήριο (το) visiting hours
	επισκέπτης (ο) visitor
ζ Z	επισκευή (η) repair
	επισκευές repairs
η H	επίσκεψη (η) visit
	ώρες επισκέψεων visiting hours
θ Θ	επιστολή (η) letter
ι I	επιστολή επείγουσα urgent or express letter
	επιστολή συστημένη registered letter
κ K	επιστροφή (η) return ; return ticket
	επιστροφή νομισμάτων returned coins
λ Λ	επιστροφές returned goods
μ M	επιταγή (η) cheque ; invoice
	ταχυδρομική επιταγή postal order
ν N	επόμενος/η/ο next
	εποχή (η) season
ξ Ξ	επτά/εφτά seven
	Επτάνησα (τα) Ionian Islands
o O	επώνυμο (το) surname ; last name
π Π	έργα (τα) works
	έργα χειρός (τα) handcrafts
ρ P	εργαλείο (το) tool
	έργο κινηματογραφικό film
σ ς Σ	εργοστάσιο (το) factory
	έργο τέχνης (το) artwork
τ T	ερώτηση (η) question
	εστιατόριο (το) restaurant
υ Y	εσώρουχα (τα) underwear ; lingerie
φ Φ	εσωτερικός/ή/ό internal
	εσωτερικού inland (on post boxes) ; domestic
	πτήσεις εσωτερικού domestic flights
χ X	εταιρ(ε)ία (η) company ; firm
ψ Ψ	έτος (το) year
	έτσι so ; like this
ω Ω	ευθεία (η) straight line
	κατ᾽ ευθείαν straight on

ευκαιρία (η) opportunity ; bargain
ευκολία (η) ease ; convenience
  ευκολίες πληρωμής credit terms
ευρωπαϊκός/ή/ό European
Ευρώπη (η) Europe
ευχαριστώ thank you
εφημερίδα (η) newspaper

ζ Z

ζάλη (η) dizziness
ζαμπόν (το) ham
ζάχαρη (η) sugar
ζαχαροπλαστείο (το) patisserie
ζέστη (η) heat
  κάνει ζέστη It's hot
ζημιά (η) damage
  πάσα ζημιά τιμωρείται anyone causing damage will be
  prosecuted
ζητώ to ask ; to seek
ζυγαριά (η) scales (for weighing)
ζυμαρικά (τα) pasta products
ζωγραφική (η) painting (art)
ζώνη (η) belt
  ζώνη ασφαλείας safety belt ; seat belt
ζώο (το) animal
ζωολογικός κήπος (ο) zoo

η H

η the (with feminine nouns)
ή or
ηλεκτρικός/ή/ό electrical
ηλεκτρισμός (ο) electricity
ηλεκτρονικός/ή/ό electronic
ηλιακός/ή/ό solar
ηλίαση (η) sunstroke
ηλικία (η) age
ηλιοθεραπεία (η) sunbathing
ήλιος (ο) sun
Ήλιος a dry white wine from Rhodes
ημέρα (η) day
ημερήσιος/α/ο daily

α A
β B
γ Γ
δ Δ
ε E
ζ Z
η H
θ Θ
ι I
κ K
λ Λ
μ M
ν N
ξ Ξ
ο O
π Π
ρ P
σ ς Σ
τ T
υ Y
φ Φ
χ X
ψ Ψ
ω Ω

ε

ζ

η

159

α Α	
β Β	
γ Γ	
δ Δ	
ε Ε	
ζ Ζ	
η Η	
θ Θ	
ι Ι	
κ Κ	
λ Λ	
μ Μ	
ν Ν	
ξ Ξ	
ο Ο	
π Π	
ρ Ρ	
σ ς Σ	
τ Τ	
υ Υ	
φ Φ	
χ Χ	
ψ Ψ	
ω Ω	

ΗΜΕΡΟΜΗΝΙΑ DATE

ημερομηνία αναχωρήσεως date of departure
ημερομηνία αφίξεως date of arrival
ημερομηνία γεννήσεως date of birth
ημερομηνία λήξεως expiry date
ημιδιατροφή (η) half board
Ηνωμένο Βασίλειο (το) United Kingdom (UK)
ΗΠΑ USA
Ηνωμένες Πολιτείες της Αμερικής United States of America
ησυχία (η) calmness ; quiet
ήσυχος/η/ο calm ; quiet

θ Θ

θάλασσα (η) sea
θαλάσσιος/α/ο of the sea
  θαλάσσιο αλεξίπτωτο paragliding
  θαλάσσιο σκι water-skiing
θέατρο (το) theatre
θέλω to want ; to need
Θεός (ο) God
θεός/θεά (ο/η) god ; goddess
Θεοτόκος (η) Virgin Mary
θεραπεία (η) treatment
θερινός/ή/ό summer
  θερινές διακοπές summer holidays
  θερινό θέρετρο summer resort
θέρμανση (η) heating
θερμίδα (η) calorie
θερμοστάτης (ο) thermostat
θέση (η) place ; seat
  διακεκριμένη θέση business class
  κράτηση θέσης seat reservation
  οικονομική θέση economy class
  πρώτη θέση first class
Θεσσαλονίκη (η) Salonica/Thessaloniki
θύελλα (η) storm
θύρα (η) gate *(airport)*
θυρίδα (η) ticket window
θυρωρείο (το) porter's lodge

ι Ι

ΙΑΗΟΥΑΡΙΟΣ JANUARY

ιατρική περίθαλψη (η) medical treatment
ιατρός (ο/η) doctor
ιδιοκτήτης/τρια (ο/η) owner

ΙΔΙΩΤΙΚΟΣ ΧΩΡΟΣ PRIVATE

ιθαγένεια (η) nationality
Ιόνιο Πέλαγος (το) Ionian sea
Ιόνιοι Νήσοι (οι) Ionian Islands

ΙΟΥΛΙΟΣ JULY

ΙΟΥΗΙΟΣ JUNE

ιππασία (η) horse riding
ιπποδρομίες (οι) horse racing
ιππόδρομος (ο) racetrack
ιππόκαμπος (ο) sea-horse
ιπτάμενο δελφίνι hydrofoil (flying dolphin)
Ισθμός της Κορίνθου Corinth canal

ΙΣΟΓΕΙΟ GROUND FLOOR

ισοτιμία (η) exchange rate
Ισπανία (η) Spain
ισπανικός/ή/ό Spanish (thing)
Ισπανός/ίδα (ο/η) Spaniard (man/woman)
ιστιοπλοΐα (η) sailing
Ιταλία (η) Italy
ιταλικός/ή/ό Italian (thing)
Ιταλός/ίδα (ο/η) Italian (man/woman)
ΙΧ private cars (parking)
ιχθυοπωλείο (το) fishmonger's

κ Κ

κάβα (η) off-licence
κάβουρας (ο) crab
καζίνο (το) casino
καθαριστήριο (το) dry-cleaner's
καθαρίστρια (η) cleaner
καθαρός/ή/ό clean

α Α
β Β
γ Γ
δ Δ
ε Ε
ζ Ζ
η Η
θ Θ
ι Ι
κ Κ
λ Λ
μ Μ
ν Ν
ξ Ξ
ο Ο
π Π
ρ Ρ
σ ς Σ
τ Τ
υ Υ
φ Φ
χ Χ
ψ Ψ
ω Ω

ι

ι

κ

K

α A	**κάθε** every ; each
	καθεδρικός ναός (ο) cathedral
β B	**καθημερινός/ή/ό** daily
	καθημερινά δρομολόγια daily departures
γ Γ	**κάθισμα** (το) seat
δ Δ	**καθολικός/ή/ό** Catholic ; total
	καθυστέρηση (η) delay
ε E	**και** and
	καιρός (ο) weather
ζ Z	**κακάο** (το) cocoa
	κακοκαιρία (η) bad weather
η H	**καλά** well ; all right
θ Θ	**καλάθι** (το) basket
	καλαμαράκια (τα) small squid (dish)
ι I	**καλαμάρι** (το) squid ; calamari
	καλημέρα good morning
κ K	**καληνύχτα** good night
λ Λ	**καλησπέρα** good evening
	καλοκαίρι (το) summer
μ M	**καλοριφέρ** (το) central heating ; radiator

K

ν N	**καλοψημένο** well done (meat)
	καλσόν (το) tights
ξ Ξ	**κάλτσα** (η) sock ; stocking
	καμαριέρα (η) chambermaid
ο O	**κάμερα** (η) camcorder
	καμπίνα (η) cabin
π Π	**κανάλι** (το) canal ; channel (TV)
	κανέλα (η) cinnamon
ρ P	**κάνω** to do
σ ς Σ	**καπέλο** (το) hat
	καπετάνιος (ο) captain (of ship)
τ T	**καπνίζω** to smoke
	μην καπνίζετε no smoking
υ Y	**καπνιστός/ή/ό** smoked
	καπνιστός σολομός smoked salmon
φ Φ	**καπνιστό χοιρινό** smoked ham
	καπνιστό ψάρι smoked fish
χ X	**καπνιστό τυρί** smoked cheese
	κάπνισμα (το) smoking
ψ Ψ	**απαγορεύεται το κάπνισμα** no smoking
	καπνιστής (ο) smoker
ω Ω	**είδη καπνιστού** tobacconist's

καπνοπωλείο (το) **tobacconist**

καπνός (ο) **smoke ; tobacco**

κάποτε **sometimes ; one time**

καράβι (το) **boat ; ship**

καραμέλα (η) **sweet(s)**

κάρβουνο (το) **coal**
στα κάρβουνα **charcoal-grilled**

καρδιά (η) **heart**

καρναβάλι (το) **carnival**

καροτσάκι (το) **pushchair**

καρπούζι (το) **watermelon**

κάρτα (η) **card ; postcard**
κάρτα απεριόριστων διαδρομών **rail card for unlimited monthly travel**
κάρτα επιβιβάσεως **boarding card**
επαγγελματική κάρτα **business card**
μόνο με κάρτα **cardholders only**
πιστωτική κάρτα **credit card**
κάρτα αναλήψεως **ATM card ; cash card**

καρτοτηλέφωνο (το) **card phone**

καρτποστάλ (η) **postcard**

καρύδα (η) **coconut**

καρύδι (το) **walnut**

καρχαρίας (ο) **shark**

κασέτα (η) **tape** (for recording)

κασετόφωνο (το) **tape recorder**

κάστανο (το) **chestnut**

κάστρο (το) **castle ; fortress**

κατάθεση (η) **deposit ; statement to police**

καταιγίδα (η) **storm**

καταλαβαίνω **to understand**
καταλαβαίνεις; **do you understand?** (familiar form)
καταλαβαίνετε; **do you understand?** (polite form)

κατάλογος (ο) **list ; menu ; directory**
τηλεφωνικός κατάλογος **telephone directory**

καταπραϋντικό (το) **tranquillizer**

κατασκήνωση (η) **camping**

κατάστημα (το) **shop**

κατάστρωμα (το) **deck**

κατεπείγον/κατεπείγουσα **urgent ; express**

κατεψυγμένος/η/ο **frozen**

κατηγορία (η) **class** (of hotel)

κατσαρόλα (η) **saucepan ; pot**

K

α Α	κατσίκα (η) goat
	κατσικάκι (το) kid *(young goat)*
β Β	κάτω under ; lower
	καύσιμα (τα) fuel
γ Γ	καφέ brown
δ Δ	καφενείο (το) coffee house
	καφές (ο) coffee *(usually Greek)*
ε Ε	καφές βαρύς γλυκός very sweet coffee
	καφές γλυκός sweet coffee
ζ Ζ	καφές μέτριος medium sweet coffee
	καφές σκέτος strong black coffee
η Η	καφές στιγμιαίος instant coffee *(Nescafé)*
	καφές φραπέ iced coffee *(Nescafé)*
θ Θ	καφετερία (η) cafeteria
	καφετιέρα (η) coffee maker
ι Ι	κέικ (το) cake ; sponge
κ Κ	κεντρικός/ή/ό central

ΚΕΝΤΡΟ CENTRE

λ Λ	
	κέντρο αλλοδαπών immigration office
μ Μ	κέντρο διασκεδάσεως nightclub
	κέντρο εκδώσεως ticket office
ν Ν	αθλητικό κέντρο sports centre
	τηλεφωνικό κέντρο telephone exchange
ξ Ξ	κεράσι (το) cherry
	Κέρκυρα (η) Corfu
ο Ο	κέρμα (το) coin
	κερνώ to buy a drink
π Π	κεφάλι (το) head
ρ Ρ	κεφτέδες (οι) meatballs
	κήπος (ο) garden
σ ς Σ	δημόσιος κήπος public garden
	ζωολογικός κήπος zoo
τ Τ	κιβώτιο (το) large box
	κιβώτιο ταχυτήτων gearbox
υ Υ	κιλό (το) kilo
	κίνδυνος (ο) danger
φ Φ	κίνδυνος θανάτου extreme danger
χ Χ	κινηματογράφος (ο) cinema
	κινητήρας (ο) engine
ψ Ψ	κίτρινος/η/ο yellow
	κλάξον (το) horn *(in car)*
ω Ω	κλειδί (το) key ; spanner

κλείνω to close

ΚΛΕΙΣΤΟ CLOSED

κλέφτης (ο) thief
κλέφτικο (το) meat dish
κλήση (η) summons
κλήση τροχαίας (η) traffic ticket
κλίμα (το) climate
κλινική (η) clinic ; hospital ; ward
κοινωνικός/ή/ό social
  κοινωνικές ασφαλίσεις national insurance
κόκκινος/η/ο red
κολοκυθάκι (το) courgette
κολοκύθι (το) marrow
κόλπος (ο) gulf ; vagina
κολύμπι (το) swimming
κολυμπώ to swim
κολώνα (η) pillar ; column
κομμωτήριο (το) hairdresser's
κομμωτής/μώτρια (ο/η) hairstylist
κομπόστα (η) stewed fruit ; compote
κομωδία (η) comedy
κονιάκ (το) cognac ; brandy
κονσέρβα (η) tinned food
κονσέρτο (το) concert
κοντά near
κόρη (η) daughter
κορίτσι (το) young girl
κόρνα (η) horn (in car)
κόσμημα (το) jewellery
κοσμηματαπωλείο (το) jewellery shop
κοστούμι (το) man's suit
κότα (η) hen
κοτολέτα (η) chop
κοτόπουλο (το) chicken
κουβέρτα (η) blanket
κουζίνα (η) kitchen ; cuisine
  ελληνική κουζίνα Greek cuisine specialities
κουνέλι (το) rabbit
κουνούπι (το) mosquito
κουνουπίδι (το) cauliflower

α A	**K**
β B	
γ Γ	
δ Δ	
ε E	
ζ Z	
η H	
θ Θ	
ι I	
κ K	
λ Λ	
μ M	**K**
ν N	
ξ Ξ	
ο O	
π Π	
ρ P	
σ ς Σ	
τ T	
υ Y	
φ Φ	
χ X	**K**
ψ Ψ	
ω Ω	

α A	κουπί (το) oar
β B	κουρείο (το) barber's shop
γ Γ	κυταλάκι (το) teaspoon
	κουτάλι (το) tablespoon
δ Δ	κουτί (το) box
	κραγιόν (το) lipstick
ε E	κρασί (το) wine
	κρασί γλυκό sweet wine
ζ Z	κρασί ξηρό dry wine
	κρασί κόκκινο red wine
η H	κρασί λευκό white wine
	κρασί ροζέ rosé wine
θ Θ	κρατήσεις (οι) bookings ; reservations
	κρατήσεις ξενοδοχείων hotel bookings
ι I	κράτηση (η) reservation
	κράτηση θέσης seat reservation
κ K	κρέας (το) meat
	κρέας αρνίσιο lamb
λ Λ	κρέας βοδινό beef
	κρέας χοιρινό pork
μ M	κρεββάτι (το) bed
ν N	κρεββατοκάμαρα (η) bedroom
	κρέμα (η) cream
ξ Ξ	κρεμμύδι (το) onion
o O	κρεοπωλείο (το) butcher's shop
	Κρήτη (η) Crete
π Π	κρουαζιέρα (η) cruise
	κρύος/α/ο cold
ρ P	κτηνιατρείο (το) veterinary surgery
	κυβερνήτης (ο) captain (of aircraft)
σ ς Σ	Κυκλάδες (οι) Cyclades (islands)
	κυκλοφορία (η) traffic ; circulation
τ T	κυλικείο (το) canteen ; cafeteria
υ Y	Κύπρος (η) Cyprus
	Κύπριος/Κυπρία (ο/η) from Cyprus ; Cypriot
φ Φ	(man/woman)
	κυρία (η) Mrs ; lady
χ X	ΚΥΡΙΑΚΗ SUNDAY
ψ Ψ	κύριος (ο) Mr ; gentleman
	κώδικας (ο) code
ω Ω	ταχυδρομικός κώδικας postcode
	τηλεφωνικός κώδικας dialling code ; area code

λ Λ

λάδι (το) oil
  λάδη ελιάς olive oil
λαϊκός/ή/ό popular ; folk
  λαϊκή αγορά market
  λαϊκή μουσική popular music
  λαϊκή τέχνη folk art
λάστιχο (το) tyre ; rubber ; elastic
λαχανικά (τα) vegetables
λαχείο (το) lottery ticket
λεμονάδα (η) lemon squash ; lemonade
λεμόνι (το) lemon
  χυμός λεμονιού lemon juice
λεξικό (το) dictionary
λεπτό (το) minute
λεπτός/ή/ό thin ; slim
λέσχη (η) club
λευκός/ή/ό white
λεφτά (τα) money
λεωφορείο (το) bus
λεωφόρος (η) avenue
λήξη (η) expiry
λιανικός/ή/ό retail
  λιανική πώληση retail sale
λίγος/η/ο a few ; a little
  λίγο ψημένο rare (meat)
λικέρ (το) liqueur
λιμάνι (το) port ; harbour
Λιμενικό Σώμα (το) coastguard
λιμήν (ο) port
λίρα (η) pound
λίτρο (το) litre
λογαριασμός (ο) bill
λουκάνικο (το) sausage
λουκανόπιτα (η) sausage pie
λουκούμι (το) Turkish delight
λύσσα (η) rabies

μ Μ

μαγαζί (το) shop
μαγειρεύω to cook

α Α	
β Β	
γ Γ	
δ Δ	
ε Ε	
ζ Ζ	
η Η	
θ Θ	
ι Ι	
κ Κ	
λ Λ	
μ Μ	
ν Ν	
ξ Ξ	
ο Ο	
π Π	
ρ Ρ	
σ ς Σ	
τ Τ	
υ Υ	
φ Φ	
χ Χ	
ψ Ψ	
ω Ω	

λ

λ

μ

μ

α A	μαγιό (το) swimsuit
β B	μαϊντανός (ο) parsley
γ Γ	ΜΑΙΟΣ MAY
δ Δ	μακαρόνια (τα) macaroni ; spaghetti dishes
ε E	μάλιστα yes ; of course
ζ Z	μαλλί (το) wool
η H	μαλλιά (τα) hair
θ Θ	μάλλινος/η/ο woollen
ι I	μαμά (η) mum
κ K	μανιτάρια (τα) mushrooms
λ Λ	μανταρίνι (το) tangerine
μ M	μαντήλι (το) handkerchief
ν N	μαξιλάρι (το) pillow ; cushion
ξ Ξ	μαργαρίνη (η) margarine
ο O	μαργαριτάρι (το) pearl
π Π	μάρμαρο (το) marble
ρ P	μαρμαρινός/ή/ό made of marble
σ ς Σ	μαρμελάδα (η) jam
τ T	μαρούλι (το) lettuce
υ Y	ΜΑΡΤΙΟΣ MARCH
φ Φ	μαύρος/η/ο black
χ X	μαχαίρι (το) knife
ψ Ψ	μαχαιροπήρουνα (τα) cutlery
ω Ω	με with

μ μεγάλος/η/ο large ; big
μέγαρο (το) hall ; palace ; block of apartments
μέγαρο μουσικής concert hall
μέγαρο αστυνομίας police headquarters
μέγεθος (το) size
μεζεδάκια (τα) selection of appetizers and salads served
as a starter *(like tapas)*
μέλι (το) honey
μελιτζάνα (η) aubergine ; eggplant
μέλος (το) member
μενού (το) menu
μέρα (η) day
μερίδα (η) portion
μέσα in ; inside
μεσάνυχτα (τα) midnight
μεσημέρι (το) midday

μ

168

Μεσόγειος (η) Mediterranean Sea
μέσω via
μετά after
μετάξι (το) silk
μεταξύ between ; among
  εν τω μεταξύ meanwhile
μεταφράζω to translate
μεταχειρισμένος/η/ο used ; second-hand
μετεωρολογικό δελτίο (το) weather forecast
μετρητά (τα) cash
μετρό (το) underground (railway)
μη... do not...
  μη καπνίζετε no smoking
  μην κόπτετε άνθη do not pick flowers
  μην πατάτε το πράσινο keep off the grass
  μη ρίπτετε σκουπίδια no dumping (rubbish)
  μη σταθμεύετε no parking
μηδέν zero
μήλο (το) apple
μηλόπιτα (η) apple pie
μήνας (o) month
  μήνας του μέλιτος honeymoon
μητέρα (η) mother
μηχανή (η) machine ; engine
μηχανικός (o) mechanic ; engineer
μία a(n) ; one (with feminine nouns)
μικρός/ή/ό small
μόδα (η) fashion
μολύβι (το) pencil
μόλυνση (η) infection ; pollution
μοναστήρι (το) monastery
μονόδρομος (o) one-way street
μονοπάτι (το) path
μόνος/η/ο alone ; only
  μόνο είσοδος/έξοδος entrance/exit only
μονός/ή/ό single ; alone
μοσχάρι (το) calf ; veal
μοτοσικλέτα (η) motorcycle

ΜΟΥΣΕΙΟ MUSEUM

  Αρχαιολογικό Μουσείο Archaeological Museum
  Μουσείο Λαϊκής Τέχνης Folk Museum
μουσική (η) music

α A
β B
γ Γ
δ Δ
ε E
ζ Z
η H
θ Θ
ι I
κ K
λ Λ
μ M
ν N
ξ Ξ
ο O
π Π
ρ P
σ ς Σ
τ T
υ Y
φ Φ
χ X
ψ Ψ
ω Ω

μ
μ
μ

α A
β B
γ Γ
δ Δ
ε E
ζ Z
η H
θ Θ
ι I
κ K
λ Λ
μ M
ν N
ξ Ξ
ο Ο
π Π
ρ Ρ
σ ς Σ
τ Τ
υ Υ
φ Φ
χ Χ
ψ Ψ
ω Ω

μ

ν

μουστάρδα (η) mustard
μπακάλης (ο) grocer
μπαμπάς (ο) dad
μπανάνα (η) banana ; bumbag
μπάνιο (το) bathroom ; bath
μπαρμπούνι (το) red mullet
μπαταρία (η) battery
μπέικον (το) bacon
μπιζέλια (τα) peas
μπίρα (η) beer
μπισκότο (το) biscuit
μπλε blue
μπλούζα (η) blouse
μπουζούκι (το) bouzouki
μπουκάλι (το) bottle
  μεγάλο μπουκάλι large bottle
  μικρό μπουκάλι half-bottle
μπουρνούζι (το) bathrobe
μπριζόλα (η) chop ; steak
μπύρα (η) beer
Μυκήναι Mycenae
Μυκηναϊκός πολιτισμός (ο) Mycenean civilization
μύτη (η) nose
μωρό (το) baby
  για μωρά for babies
μωσαϊκό (το) mosaic

ν Ν

ναι yes
ναός (ο) temple ; church
  καθεδρικός ναός cathedral
ναύλο (το) fare
νάυλον nylon
ναυλωμένος/η/ο chartered
  ναυλωμένη πτήση charter flight
ναυτία (η) travel sickness
ναυτικός όμιλος (ο) sailing club
ναυτιλιακά yacht chandler
νεκρός/ή/ό dead
νεκροταφείο (το) cemetery
νεοελληνικά (τα) Modern Greek
νερό (το) water

επιτραπέζιο νερό still mineral water
μεταλλικό νερό mineral water
πόσιμο νερό drinking water
νεφρός (ο) kidney
νεωτερισμός (ο) improvement ; novelty
νηπιαγωγείο (το) nursery school
νησί (το) island
νησίδα (η) traffic island
νίκη (η) victory

NOEMBΡΙΟΣ NOVEMBER

νοίκι (το) rent
νόμισμα (το) coin ; currency
  επιστροφή νομισμάτων returned coins
νομισματοδέχτης (ο) coin-operated phone
νοσοκομείο (το) hospital
νοσοκόμος/α (ο/η) nurse
νότιος/α/ο southern
νότος (ο) south
ντομάτα (η) tomato
ντουζίνα (η) dozen
ντους (το) shower *(in bath)*
νύκτα/νύχτα (η) night
νυκτερινός/ή/ό all-night *(chemists, etc)*

ξ Ξ

ξεναγός (ο/η) guide
ξενοδοχείο (το) hotel
  κρατήσεις ξενοδοχείων hotel reservations
ξένος/η/ο strange ; foreign
  ξένος/η (ο/η) foreigner ; visitor
ξενώνας (ο) guesthouse
ξεχνώ to forget
ξηρός/ή/ό dry
  ξηροί καρποί dried fruit and nuts
ξιφίας (ο) swordfish
ξύδι (το) vinegar
ξύλο (το) wood
ξυριστική μηχανή (η) safety razor

α A
β B
γ Γ
δ Δ
ε E
ζ Z
η H
θ Θ
ι I
κ K
λ Λ
μ M
ν N
ξ Ξ
ο O
π Π
ρ P
σ ς Σ
τ T
υ Y
φ Φ
χ X
ψ Ψ
ω Ω

ν

ν

ξ

α A
β B
γ Γ
δ Δ
ε E
ζ Z
η H
θ Θ
ι I
κ K
λ Λ
μ M
ν N
ξ Ξ
ο O
π Π
ρ P
σ ς Σ
τ T
υ Y
φ Φ
χ X
ψ Ψ
ω Ω

ο O

οδηγία (η) instruction
  οδηγίες χρήσεως instructions for use
οδηγός (ο) driver ; guidebook
οδηγώ to drive
οδική βοήθεια (η) breakdown service
οδοντιατρείο (το) dental surgery
οδοντίατρος (ο/η) dentist
οδοντόβουρτσα (η) toothbrush
οδοντόκρεμα (η) toothpaste
οδοντοστοιχία (η) denture(s)
οδός (η) road ; street
οικογένεια (η) family
οικονομική θέση (η) economy class
οίκος (ο) house
  οίκος μόδας fashion house
οινομαγειρείον (το) licensed restaurant with traditional
  cuisine
οινοπνευματώδη ποτά (τα) spirits
οίνος (ο) wine
οκτώ/οχτώ eight

ΟΚΤΩΒΡΙΟΣ October

ολισθηρόν οδόστρωμα (το) slippery road surface
όλος/η/ο all of
Ολυμπία (η) Olympia
ολυμπιακός/ή/ό Olympic
  Ολυμπιακή Αεροπορία Olympic Airways
  Ολυμπιακό Στάδιο Olympic stadium
  Ολυμπιακοί Αγώνες Olympic games
Όλυμπος (ο) Mount Olympus
ομελέτα (η) omelette
όμιλος (ο) club
  ναυτικός όμιλος sailing club
ομπρέλα (η) umbrella
όνομα (το) name
ονοματεπώνυμο (το) full name
όπερα (η) opera
οπτικός οίκος (ο) optician's
οργανισμός (ο) organization
  Οργανισμός Σιδηροδρόμων Ελλάδος (ΟΣΕ) Greek
  Railways

172

οργανωμένος/η/ο organized
  οργανωμένα ταξίδια organized tours
ορεκτικό (το) starter ; appetizer
όρεξη (η) appetite
  καλή όρεξη enjoy your meal!
ορθόδοξος/η/ο orthodox
όρος (ο) condition
  όροι ενοικιάσεως conditions of hire
όρος (το) mountain
όροφος (ο) floor ; storey
ΟΣΕ Greek Railways
ΟΤΕ Greek Telecom
ουδέν:ουδέν προς δήλωση nothing to declare
ούζο (το) ouzo
ουρά (η) tail ; queue
όχι no

π Π

παγάκι (το) ice cube
παϊδάκι (το) lamb chop
πάγος (ο) ice
παγωμένος/η/ο frozen
παγωτό (το) ice cream
παιδικός/ή/ό for children
  παιδικά childrens wear
  παιδικός σταθμός crèche
πακέτο (το) parcel ; packet
παλτό (το) coat
πάνα (η) nappy
Παναγία (η) the Virgin Mary
πανεπιστήμιο (το) university
πανσιόν (η) guesthouse
πάντα/πάντοτε always
παντελόνι (το) trousers
παντοπωλείο (το) grocer's
παπάς (ο) priest
πάπλωμα (το) duvet
παππούς (ο) grandfather
παπούτσι (το) shoe
παραγγελία (η) order
παραγγέλνω to order
παραγωγή (η) production

α Α	
β Β	
γ Γ	
δ Δ	
ε Ε	
ζ Ζ	
η Η	
θ Θ	
ι Ι	
κ Κ	
λ Λ	
μ Μ	
ν Ν	π
ξ Ξ	
ο Ο	
π Π	
ρ Ρ	
σ ς Σ	
τ Τ	
υ Υ	
φ Φ	
χ Χ	
ψ Ψ	π
ω Ω	

π	
α Α	Ελληνικής παραγωγής produce of Greece
	παράθυρο (το) window
β Β	παρακαλώ please
	παρακαμπτήριος (ο) by-pass
γ Γ	παραλία (η) seashore ; beach
δ Δ	ΠΑΡΑΣΚΕΥΗ Friday
ε Ε	παράσταση (η) performance
	παρέα (η) company ; group
ζ Ζ	Παρθενών/ώνας (ο) the Parthenon
η Η	πάρκο (το) park
	παρμπρίζ (το) windscreen
θ Θ	πάστα (η) pastry ; cake
	παστέλι (το) honey and sesame seed bar
ι Ι	Πάσχα (το) Easter
	πατάτα (η) potato
κ Κ	πατάτες πουρέ creamed/mashed potatoes
	πατάτες τηγανητές chips
λ Λ	πατάτες φούρνου roast potatoes
	πατέρας (ο) father
μ Μ	παυσίπονο (το) painkiller
π ν Ν	πάω to go
	πέδιλα (τα) sandals
ξ Ξ	πεζοδρόμιο (το) pavement
ο Ο	ΠΕΖΟΔΡΟΜΟΣ PEDESTRIAN AREA
π Π	πεζός (ο) pedestrian
	Πειραιάς/Πειραιεύς (ο) Piraeus
ρ Ρ	πελάτης/τρια (ο/η) customer
	Πελοπόννησος (η) Peloponnese
σ ς Σ	ΠΕΜΠΤΗ Thursday
τ Τ	πένα (η) pen ; pence
	πεπόνι (το) melon
υ Υ	περιοδικό (το) magazine
	περιοχή (η) area
φ Φ	περίπατος (ο) walk
χ Χ	περίπτερο (το) kiosk
	περιστέρι (το) pigeon ; dove
π ψ Ψ	πέτρα (η) stone
	πετρέλαιο (το) diesel fuel
ω Ω	πετρινός/ή/ό made of stone

174

πετσέτα (η) towel
πεύκο (το) pine tree
πηγαίνω to go
πιάτο (το) plate ; dish

ΠΙΕΣΑΤΕ push

πίεση (η) pressure
  πίεση αίματος blood pressure
πιλότος (ο) pilot
πινακίδα (η) sign ; number plate
  πινακίδα κυκλοφορίας number plate
πινακοθήκη (η) art gallery ; collection of paintings
πίπα (η) pipe
πιπέρι (το) pepper
  πιπεριές γεμιστές stuffed peppers
πισίνα (η) swimming pool
πιστοποιητικό (το) certificate
πιστωτική κάρτα (η) credit card
πίσω behind ; back
πίτα (η) pie
πιτζάμες (οι) pyjamas
πίτσα (η) pizza
πιτσαρία (η) pizzeria
πλαζ (η) beach
πλάι next to
πλατεία (η) square
πλατίνες (οι) points (in car)
πλεκτά (τα) knitwear

ΠΛΗΡΟΦΟΡΙΕΣ INFORMATION

πληροφορίες δρομολογίων travel information
πλήρωμα (το) crew
  τα μέλη του πληρώματος crew members
πληρωμή (η) payment
  ευκολίες πληρωμής credit facilities
  προς πληρωμή insert money
πληρώνω to pay
πλοίο (το) ship
πλυντήριο (το) washing machine
  πλυντήριο αυτοκινήτων car wash
  πλυντήριο πιάτων dish washer
ποδηλάτης (ο) cyclist
ποδήλατο (το) bicycle

α A
β B
γ Γ
δ Δ
ε E
ζ Z
η H
θ Θ
ι I
κ K
λ Λ
μ M
ν N
ξ Ξ
ο O
π Π
ρ P
σ ς Σ
τ T
υ Y
φ Φ
χ X
ψ Ψ
ω Ω

π

π

π

175

α Α	ποδήλατο της θάλασσας pedalo
β Β	πόδι (το) foot ; leg
	ποδόσφαιρο (το) football
γ Γ	ποιος/ποια/ποιο which
	πόλη/ις (η) town ; city
δ Δ	πολυκατάστημα (το) department store
	πολυκατοικία (η) block of flats
ε Ε	πολύς/πολλή/πολύ many ; much
ζ Ζ	πονόδοντος (ο) toothache
	πονοκέφαλος (ο) headache
η Η	πονόλαιμος (ο) sore throat
	πόνος (ο) pain
θ Θ	πόρτα (η) door
	πορτοκαλάδα (η) orange squash
ι Ι	πορτοκάλι (το) orange
	χυμός πορτοκαλιού orange juice
κ Κ	πορτοφόλι (το) wallet
λ Λ	πόσα; how many?
	πόσο; how much?
μ Μ	πόσο κάνει; how much is it?
	πόσο κοστίζει; how much does it cost?
ν Ν	ποσοστό (το) rate ; percentage
	ποσοστό υπηρεσίας service charge
ξ Ξ	συμπεριλαμβανομένου ποσοστού υπηρεσίας service
	included
ο Ο	ποσότητα (η) quantity
π Π	πότε; when?
	ποτέ never
ρ Ρ	ποτήρι (το) glass (for drinking)
	ποτό (το) drink
σ ς Σ	πού; where?
	πουκάμισο (το) shirt
τ Τ	πούλμαν (το) coach
	πουλώ to sell
υ Υ	πουρμπουάρ (το) tip (to waiter, etc)
	πούρο (το) cigar
φ Φ	πράκτορας (ο) agent
χ Χ	πρακτορείο (το) agency
	πράσινος/η/ο green
ψ Ψ	πρατήριο (το) specialist shop
	πρατήριο βενζίνης petrol station
ω Ω	πρατήριο άρτου baker's

πρεσβεία (η) embassy
πρίζα (η) plug ; socket
πριν before
προβολέας (ο) headlight
πρόγευμα (το) breakfast
πρόγραμμα (το) programme
πρόεδρος (ο) president
  προεδρικό μέγαρο presidential palace
προειδοποίηση (η) warning
προέλευση (η) embarkation point
προϊόν (το) product
  Ελληνικό προϊόν product of Greece
προκαταβολή (η) deposit
προκρατήσεις (οι) advance bookings
προξενείο (το) consulate
πρόξενος (ο) consul
προορισμός (ο) destination
προπληρώνω to pay in advance
Προ-πο (το) Greek football pools
προσγείωση (η) landing
προσδεθείτε fasten safety belts
πρόσκληση (η) invitation
προσοχή (η) attention
προτεστάντης (ο) protestant
πρόστιμο (το) fine
πρόχειρος/η/ο handy ; impromptu
  πρόχειρο φαγητό snack
πρωί (το) morning
πρωινός/ή/ό morning
πρωινό (το) breakfast
πρωτεύουσα (η) capital city
πρωτομαγιά (η) May Day
πρώτος/η/ο first
  πρώτες βοήθειες casualty (hospital)
  πρώτη θέση first class
πρωτοχρονιά (η) New Years Day
πτήση (η) flight
  πτήσεις εξωτερικού international flights
  πτήσεις εσωτερικού domestic flights
  αριθμός πτήσης flight number
  ναυλωμένη πτήση charter flight
  τακτικές πτήσεις scheduled flights

α A
β B
γ Γ
δ Δ
ε E
ζ Z
η H
θ Θ
ι I
κ K
λ Λ
μ M
ν N
ξ Ξ
ο O
π Π
ρ P
σ ς Σ
τ T
υ Y
φ Φ
χ X
ψ Ψ
ω Ω

α Α	
β Β	
γ Γ	
δ Δ	
ε Ε	
ζ Ζ	
η Η	
θ Θ	
ι Ι	
κ Κ	
λ Λ	
μ Μ	
ν Ν	
ξ Ξ	
ο Ο	
π Π	
ρ Ρ	
σ ς Σ	
τ Τ	
υ Υ	
φ Φ	
χ Χ	
ψ Ψ	
ω Ω	

πυρκαγιά (η) **fire**
πυροσβεστήρας (ο) **fire extinguisher**
πυροσβέστης (ο) **fireman**
πυροσβεστική (η) **fire brigade**
  πυροσβεστική υπηρεσία **fire brigade**
  πυροσβεστικός σταθμός **fire station**
πώληση (η) **sale**
  λιανική πώληση **retail sale**
  χονδρική πώληση **wholesale**
πωλητής/ήτρια(ο/η) **sales assistant**

ΠΩΛΕΙΤΑΙ FOR SALE

πώς; **how?**

ρ Ρ

ρεζέρβα (η) **spare wheel**
ρέστα (τα) **change** (money)
ρετσίνα (η) **retsina**
ρεύμα (το) **current ; electricity**
ρόδα (η) **wheel**
ροδάκινο (το) **peach**
ρόδι (το) **pomegranate**
Ρόδος (η) **Rhodes (island)**
ρολόι (το) **watch ; clock**
ρούμι (το) **rum**
ρύζι (το) **rice**
ρυμουλκώ **to tow away**

σ ς Σ

ΣΑΒΒΑΤΟ Saturday

Σαββατοκύριακο (το) **weekend**
σακάκι (το) **jacket** (menswear)
σαλάμι (το) **salami**
σαλάτα (η) **salad**
σαλιγκάρι (το) **snail**
σάλτσα (η) **sauce**
σαμπάνια (η) **champagne**
σαμπουάν (το) **shampoo**
σάντουιτς (το) **sandwich**
σαπούνι (το) **soap**
σβήνω **to extinguish**

σβήσατε τα τσιγάρα σας extinguish cigarettes

ΣΕΠΤΕΜΒΡΙΟΣ September

σέρβις (το) service
σεφ (ο) chef
σήμα (το) sign ; signal
   σήμα κατατεθέν trademark
   σήμα κινδύνου emergency signal
σήμερα today
σιγά slowly
σιγή (η) silence
σιδηρόδρομος (ο) railway
   σιδηροδρομικός σταθμός railway station
   σιδηροδρομικώς by rail
σιεφταλιά (η) spicy meat kebab
σκάλα (η) ladder ; staircase
σκαλί (το) step
σκέτος/η/ο plain
   καφές σκέτος black coffee
σκηνή (η) tent ; stage
σκι (το) ski
   θαλάσσιο σκι water-skiing
σκοινί (το) rope
σκορδαλιά (η) garlic sauce
σκόρδο (ο) garlic
σκουπίδια (τα) rubbish ; refuse
σκυλί (το) dog
Σκωτία (η) Scotland
σκωτσέζικος/η/ο (η) Scottish (thing)
Σκωτσέζος/Σκωτσέζα (ο/η) Scotsman/Scotswoman
σόδα (η) soda
σοκολάτα (η) chocolate
σολομός (ο) salmon
σόμπα (η) stove ; heater
σούβλα (η) skewer
σουβλάκι (το) meat cooked on skewer
σούπα (η) soup
σοφέρ(ο) chauffeur
σπανάκι (το) spinach
σπανακόπιτα (η) spinach pie
σπαράγγι (το) asparagus
σπεσιαλιτέ της κουζίνας todays special dish

α A
β B
γ Γ
δ Δ
ε E
ζ Z
η H
θ Θ
ι I
κ K
λ Λ
μ M
ν N
ξ Ξ
ο O
π Π
ρ P
σ ς Σ
τ T
υ Y
φ Φ
χ X
ψ Ψ
ω Ω

σ

σ

σ

α A	σπίρτο (το) match
β B	σπίτι (το) house ; home
	σπιτικός/ή/ο homemade
γ Γ	σπορ (τα) sports
δ Δ	Σποράδες (οι) the Sporades
ε E	στάδιο (το) stadium ; stage
	σταθμεύω to park
ζ Z	ανώτατος χρόνος σταθμεύσεως maximum parking time
	απαγορεύεται η στάθμευση no parking
η H	μη σταθμεύετε no parking
	χώρος σταθμεύσεως parking area
θ Θ	σταθμός (ο) station
	πυροσβεστικός σταθμός fire station
ι I	σιδηροδρομικός σταθμός railway station
	σταθμός υπεραστικών λεωφορείων bus station (intercity)
κ K	στάση/σις (η) stop
	στάση εργασίας strike
λ Λ	στάσις ΗΛΠΑΠ trolley bus stop
	στάση λεωφορείου bus stop
μ M	σταυροδρόμι (το) crossroads
	σταφίδα (η) raisin
ν N	σταφύλι (το) grape
	στεγνοκαθαριστήριο (το) dry-cleaner's
ξ Ξ	στιγμή (η) moment
	στοά (η) arcade
ο O	στροφή (η) turn ; bend
	στρώμα (το) mattress
π Π	συγγνώμη sorry ; excuse me
	συγκοινωνία (η) public transport
ρ P	συγχαρητήρια congratulations
	συγχωρώ:με συγχωρείτε excuse me
σ ς Σ	σύζυγος (ο/η) husband/wife
τ T	σύκο (το) fig
	συκώτι (το) liver
υ Y	συμπεριλαμβάνω to include
	συμπλέκτης (ο) clutch (of car)
φ Φ	συμπληρώνω to fill in
	σύμπτωμα (το) symptom
χ X	συμφωνία (η) agreement
	συμφωνώ to agree
ψ Ψ	συνάλλαγμα (το) foreign exchange
	δήλωση συναλλάγματος currency declaration
ω Ω	η τιμή του συναλλάγματος exchange rate

συνάντηση (η) meeting
συναντώ to meet
συναυλία (η) concert
συνεργείο (το) workshop ; garage for car repairs
  συνεργείο αυτοκινήτων car repairs
σύνθεση (η) ingredients ; flower arrangement
σύνολο (το) total
σύνορα (τα) border ; frontier
συνταγή (η) prescription ; recipe

ΣΥΡΑΤΕ PULL

σύστημα κλιματισμού (το) air conditioning
συστημένη επιστολή (η) registered letter
συχνά often
σφράγισμα (το) filling (in tooth)
σχηματίζω to form
  σχηματίστε τον αριθμό dial the number
σχολείο (το) school
σχολή (η) school
  σχολή οδηγών driving school
  σχολή σκι ski school
σώζω to save ; to rescue
σώμα (το) body
σωσίβιο (το) life jacket

τ T

ταβέρνα (η) tavern with traditional food and wine
ταινία (η) film ; strip ; tape

ΤΑΜΕΙΟ CASH DESK

ταμίας (ο/η) cashier
ταμιευτήριο (το) savings bank
ταξί (το) taxi
  αγοραίο ταξί minicab (no meter)
  γραφείο ταξί taxi office
  ραδιό ταξί radio taxi
ταξίδι (το) journey ; tour
  καλό ταξίδι have a good trip
  ταξιδιωτικό γραφείο travel agent
  οργανωμένα ταξίδια organized tours
ταξιθέτης/τρια (ο/η) theatre attendant
ταραμοσαλάτα (η) taramosalata
ταυτότητα (η) identity ; identity card

α A	ταχεία (η) **express train**
β B	ταχυδρομείο (το) **post office** Ελληνικά Ταχυδρομεία (ΕΛΤΑ) **Greek Post Office**
γ Γ	ταχυδρομικά (τέλη) **postage** ταχυδρομικές επιταγές **postal orders**
δ Δ	ταχυδρομικός κώδικας **postcode** ταχυδρομικώς **by post**
ε E	ταχύμετρο (το) **speedometer**
ζ Z	ταχύτητα/ταχύτης (η) **speed** κιβώτιο ταχυτήτων **gearbox**
η H	τελευταίος/α/ο **last**
θ Θ	τέλος (το) **end ; tax ; duty** ταχυδρομικά τέλη **postage** οδικά τέλη **road tax** τέλος πάντων **well** (to start sentence)
ι I	τελωνείο (το) **customs**
κ K	τένις (το) **tennis**
λ Λ	τέντα (η) **tent** τέρμα (το) **terminus ; end of route**
μ M	**ΤΕΤΑΡΤΗ Wednesday**
ν N	τέχνη (η) **art** λαϊκή τέχνη **folk art**
ξ Ξ	τεχνητώς κεχρωσμένο **artificial colourings**
o O	τζαμί (το) **mosque ; glass** (of window) τζατζίκι (το) **tsatsiki** (yoghurt, cucumber and garlic)
π Π	τηγανίτα (η) **pancake** τηλεγραφείο (το) **telegraph office**
ρ P	τηλεγράφημα (το) **telegram** τηλεκάρτα (η) **phonecard**
σ ς Σ	τηλεόραση (η) **television** τηλεπικοινωνίες (οι) **telecommunications**
τ T	τηλεφώνημα (το) **telephone call**
υ Y	**ΤΗΛΕΦΩΝΟ TELEPHONE**
φ Φ	τηλεφωνικός θάλαμος **phone box** τηλεφωνικός κατάλογος **telephone directory** τηλεφωνικός κώδικας **dialling code ; area code**
χ X	τι; **what?** τι είναι; **what is it?**
ψ Ψ	τιμή (η) **price ; honour** τιμή εισιτηρίου **price of ticket ; fare**
ω Ω	τιμοκατάλογος (ο) **price list**

τιμολόγιο (το) invoice
τιμόνι (το) steering wheel
τιμωρώ to punish
τίποτα nothing
τμήμα (το) department ; police station
το it ; the *(with neuter nouns)*
τοιχοκόλληση (η) bill posting
τόκος (ο) interest *(bank)*
τόνος (ο) ton ; tuna fish
τοστ (το) toasted sandwich

ΤΟΥΑΛΕΤΕΣ TOILETS

τουρισμός (ο) tourism
τουρίστας/στρια (ο/η) tourist
τουριστικός/ή/ό tourist
  τουριστικά είδη souvenirs
  τουριστική αστυνομία Tourist Police
Τουρκία (η) Turkey
τραγούδι (το) song
τραγωδία (η) tragedy
τράπεζα (η) bank
τραπεζαρία (η) dining room
τραπέζι (το) table
τρένο (το) train

ΤΡΙΤΗ Tuesday

τρόλεϋ (το) trolley bus
τροφή (η) food
τροχαία (η) traffic police
τροχός (ο) wheel
τροχόσπιτο (το) caravan
τροχοφόρο (το) vehicle
τρώγω/τρώω to eat
τσάι (το) tea
τσάντα (η) bag
τσιγάρο (το) cigarette
τυρί (το) cheese
τυρόπιτα (η) cheese pie
τυφλός/ή/ό blind

α Α	
β Β	
γ Γ	
δ Δ	
ε Ε	
ζ Ζ	
η Η	
θ Θ	
ι Ι	
κ Κ	
λ Λ	
μ Μ	
ν Ν	
ξ Ξ	
ο Ο	
π Π	
ρ Ρ	
σ ς Σ	
τ Τ	
υ Υ	
φ Φ	
χ Χ	
ψ Ψ	
ω Ω	

α A
β B
γ Γ
δ Δ
ε E
ζ Z
η H
θ Θ
ι I
κ K
λ Λ
μ M
ν N
ξ Ξ
ο O
π Π
ρ P
σ ς Σ
τ T
υ Y
φ Φ
χ X
ψ Ψ
ω Ω

υ Y

υγεία (η) health
  στην υγειά σας your health ; cheers
υγειονομικός έλεγχος (ο) health inspection
Ύδρα (η) Hydra (island)
Υμηττός (ο) Mount Hymettos
υπεραγορά (η) supermarket
υπεραστικό λεωφορείο (το) long-distance coach
υπερωκεάνειο (το) liner
υπήκοος (ο/η) citizen
υπηκόοτης/υπηκοότητα (η) nationality
υπηρεσία (η) service
  ποσοστό υπηρεσίας service charge
υπηρέτης (ο) servant
υπηρέτρια (η) maid
υπόγειος/α/ο underground
  υπόγεια διάβαση πεζών pedestrian subway
  υπόγειος σιδηρόδρομος underground (railway)
υποδοχή (η) reception
  χώρος υποδοχής reception area
υπολογιστής (ο) computer
υποκατάστημα (το) branch office
υπουργείο (το) ministry
υψηλός/ή/ό high
  υψηλή τάση high voltage
ύφασμα (το) fabric ; cloth
  υφάσματα textiles
  υφάσματα επιπλώσεων upholstery fabrics
ύψος (το) height
  ύψος περιορισμένο height limit

φ Φ

φαγητό (το) food ; meal
φαΐ (το) food
φακός (ο) lens ; torch
  φακοί επαφής contact lenses
φανάρι (το) traffic light ; lantern
φαξ (το) fax
φαρμακείο (το) chemist's
φαρμάκι (το) poison
φάρμακο (το) medicine
φάρος (ο) lighthouse

φασολάκι (το) green bean
φασόλι (το) haricot bean
φάω to eat

ΦΕΒΡΟΥΑΡΙΟΣ FEBRUARY

φεριμπότ (το) ferry boat
φέτα (η) feta cheese ; slice
φιλενάδα (η) girlfriend
φιλέτο (το) fillet of meat
φιλμ (το) film
  εμφανίσεις φιλμ film developing
φιλοδώρημα (το) tip ; service charge
φίλος/η (ο/η) friend
φίλτρο (το) filter
  φίλτρο αέρος air filter
  φίλτρο λαδιού oil filter
  καφές φίλτρου filter coffee
φλας (το) flash (camera)
φοιτητής/φοιτήτρια (ο/η) student
φοιτητικό εισιτήριο (το) student fare
φόρεμα (το) dress
φορολογημένα είδη duty-paid goods
φόρος (ο) tax
  συμπεριλαμβανομένων φόρων including taxes
φουντούκι (το) hazelnut
φούρνος (ο) oven ; bakery
φουσκωτά σκάφη (τα) inflatable boats
ΦΠΑ (ο) VAT
φράουλα (η) strawberry
φρένο (το) brake (in car)
φρέσκος/ια/ο fresh
φρούτο (το) fruit
φρουτοσαλάτα (η) fruit salad
φύλακας (ο) guard
φύλαξη αποσκευών (η) left-luggage office
φυστίκι (το) peanut
  φυστίκια Αιγίνης pistachio nuts
φυτό (το) plant
φως (το) light
φωτιά (η) fire
φωτογραφία (η) photograph
  έγχρωμες φωτογραφίες colour photographs

α A	φ
β B	
γ Γ	
δ Δ	
ε E	
ζ Z	
η H	
θ Θ	
ι I	
κ K	
λ Λ	
μ M	
ν N	φ
ξ Ξ	
ο O	
π Π	
ρ P	
σ ς Σ	
τ T	
υ Y	
φ Φ	
χ X	
ψ Ψ	φ
ω Ω	

185

φ

α Α	**φωτογραφίζω** to take photographs
β Β	**μη φωτογραφίζετε** no photographs
γ Γ	**φωτογραφική μηχανή (η)** camera
δ Δ	**φωτοτυπία (η)** photocopy

χ Χ

ε Ε	**χαίρετε** hello *(polite)*
ζ Ζ	**χάπι (το)** pill
	χάρτης (ο) map
η Η	**οδικός χάρτης** road map
	χαρτί (το) paper
θ Θ	**χαρτί κουζίνας** kitchen paper
ι Ι	**χαρτικά (τα)** stationery
κ Κ	**χαρτονόμισμα (το)** banknote
	χαρτοπωλείο (το) stationer's shop
λ Λ	**χασάπικο (το)** butcher's shop
μ Μ	**χειροποίητος/η/ο** handmade
	χειρούργος (ο) surgeon
ν Ν	**χειρόφρενο (το)** handbrake
ξ Ξ	**χέρι (το)** hand
	χιλιόμετρο (το) kilometre
ο Ο	**χιόνι (το)** snow
	χοιρινό (το) pork
π Π	**χορός (ο)** dance
ρ Ρ	**χορτοφάγος (ο/η)** vegetarian
	χορωδία (η) choir
σ ς Σ	**χουρμάς (ο)** date *(fruit)*
τ Τ	**χρειάζομαι** to need
	χρήματα (τα) money
υ Υ	**χρηματοκιβώτιο (το)** safe *(for valuables)*
φ Φ	**χρήση (η)** use
	οδηγίες χρήσεως instructions for use
χ Χ	**χρήσιμος/η/ο** useful
ψ Ψ	**χρητιμοποιώ** to use
ω Ω	**χριστιανός/ή** Christian
	Χριστούγεννα (τα) Christmas
	Καλά Χριστούγεννα Merry Christmas
	χρόνος (ο) time ; year
	χρυσαφικά (τα) jewellery
	χρυσός/ή/ό (made of) gold
	Χρυσός Οδηγός Yellow Pages
	χταπόδι (το) octopus

χτένα (η) comb
χτες yesterday
χυμός (ο) juice
  χυμός λεμονιού lemon juice
  χυμός πορτοκαλιού orange juice
χώρα (η) country
χωριάτικο ψωμί (το) bread *(round, flat loaf)*
χωριό (το) village
χωρίς without
  χωρίς εισπράκτορα exact fare ; prepaid ticket
χώρος (ο) area ; site
  αρχαιολογικός χώρος archaeological site
  ιδιωτικός χώρος private
  χώρος σταθμεύσεως parking area

ψ Ψ

ψάρεμα (το) fishing
ψαρεύω to fish
ψάρι (το) fish
ψαρόβαρκα (η) fishing boat
ψαροταβέρνα (η) fish tavern
ψημένος/η/ο cooked ; roasted ; grilled
ψητός/ή/ό roast ; grilled
ψυγείο (το) fridge
ψυχώ to cool
ψωμάς (ο) baker
ψωμί (το) bread

ω Ω

ΩΘΗΣΑΤΕ PUSH

ωτοστόπ (το) hitchhiking
ώρα (η) time ; hour
  ώρες επισκέψεως visiting hours
  ώρες λειτουργίας opening hours
  ώρες συναλλαγής banking hours
  της ώρας freshly cooked *(food)*
ωραίος/α/ο beautiful
ωράριο (το) timetable
ως as
ωστόσο however
ωφέλιμος/η/ο useful
ωφελώ to be useful

NOUNS

Greek nouns can be *masculine, feminine* or *neuter* and the words for
the and **a** (articles) change according to the gender of the noun.

ένας *(enas)*	= **a** with *masculine* nouns
μία *(meea)*	= **a** with *feminine* nouns
ένα *(ena)*	= **a** with *neuter* nouns
ο *(o)*	= **the** with *masculine* nouns
η *(ee)*	= **the** with *feminine* nouns
το *(to)*	= **the** with *neuter* nouns

The article is the most reliable indication of the gender of a noun,
i.e. whether it is *masculine, feminine* or *neuter*.

In the dictionary sections you will come across examples like this:
ο / η γιατρός *(yatros)* **doctor**. This means that the same ending is
used for men as well as women doctors i.e. **ο γιατρός** is a male
doctor, **η γιατρός** is a female doctor.

You will also encounter entries like **ο Άγγλος / η Αγγλίδα** indicat-
ing that an **Englishman** is referred to as **ο Άγγλος** *(anglos)* while
an **Englishwoman** is **η Αγγλίδα** *(angleedha)*.

The most common endings of *masculine* nouns are **-ος** *(os)*,
-ας *(as)*, **-ης** *(ees)*, e.g.

ο καιρός *(keros)*	**weather**
ο πατέρας *(pateras)*	**father**
ο κυβερνήτης *(keeverneetees)*	**captain** *(of aeroplane)*

The most common endings of *feminine* nouns are **-α** *(a)*,
-η *(ee)*, e.g.

η μητέρα *(meetera)*	**mother**
η Κρήτη *(kreetee)*	**Crete**

The most common *neuter* endings are: **-ο** *(o)*, **-ι** *(ee)*, e.g.

το κτίριο *(kteereeo)*	**building**
το πορτοκάλι *(portokalee)*	**orange** *(fruit)*

PLURALS

The article **the** changes in the plural. For *masculine* (**ο**) and *feminine* (**η**) nouns it becomes **οι** *(ee)*. For *neuter* nouns (**το**) it
becomes **τα** *(ta)*.

Nouns have different endings in the plural. *Masculine* nouns
change their endings to **-οι** *(ee)*, *feminine* nouns change their
endings to **-ες** *(es)*.

ο βράχος *(vrakhos)*   οι βράχοι *(vrakhee)*

η κυρία *(kereea)*   οι κυρίες *(keree-es)*

Neuter nouns change their endings to **-α** *(a)*

το κτίριο *(kteereeo)*   τα κτίρια *(kteereea)*

There are many exceptions to the above rules such as:

ο άντρας *(andras)*   οι άντρες *(andres)*

ADJECTIVES

Adjective endings must agree with the gender and number of the
noun they describe, e.g.

ο καλός πατέρας *(kalos pateras)*	**the good father**
η καλή κυρία *(kalee kereea)*	**the good lady**
οι καλοί πατέρες *(kalee pateres)*	**the good fathers**
οι καλές κυρίες *(kales keree-es)*	**the good ladies**

You will see that in the Greek-English dictionary section of this
book, all adjectives are given with their endings clearly marked
e.g. **κρύος/α/ο** *(kreeos/a/o)*   **cold**

By far the most common adjectival endings are **-ος** *(os)* for masculine, **-η** *(ee)* for *feminine* and **-ο** *(o)* for *neuter* nouns.
e.g. **καλος/η/ο** *(kalos/ee/o)*   **cold**

In Greek, adjectives *precede* the noun they describe.

POSSESSIVE ADJECTIVES

In Greek the possessive adjective – my, your, his, etc. follow the
noun. And they don't change even if the noun is *masculine*, *feminine*, *singular* or *plural*. The article will still go in front of the noun.

my	μου	*moo*	**our**	μας	*mas*
your	σου	*soo*	**your**	σας	*sas**
his	του	*too*	**their**	τους	*toos*
her	της	*tees*			
its	του	*too*			

*This is also the polite form

my key	το κλειδί μου	*to kleedhee moo*
your room	το δωμάτιο σας	*to dhomateeo sas*

VERBS

The most essential verbs in Greek are the verbs εἰμαι **I am** and
ἔχω **I have**. Unlike verbs in English, Greek verbs have a different
ending for each person and
number.

to be

εἰμαι	I am	*ee*me
εἰσαι	you are	*ee*se
εἰναι	he/she/it is	*ee*ne
εἰμαστε	we are	*ee*maste
εἰστε	you are	*ee*ste*
εἰναι	they are	*ee*ne

* This form is also used when addressing people we don't know
well, and referred to as the polite plural (like the French 'vous').

NOTE: While in English it is necessary to use the personal pronoun
i.e. **we**, **you** etc, in order to distinguish between **we are**, **you are**
etc, in Greek this function is carried out by the different endings of
the verb itself. This way in Greek, **we are** and **they are** can be
simply εἰμαστε *(eemaste)*, εἰναι *(eene)*.

to have

ἔχω	I have	*e*kho
ἔχεις	you have	*e*khees
ἔχει	he/she/it has	*e*khee
ἔχουμε	we have	*e*khoome
ἔχετε	you have	*e*khete
ἔχουν	they have	*e*khoon

NOTE As above, **I have** can be expressed in Greek with simply the
verb ἔχω ; each ending is particular to a specific person.
Verbs in Greek in the active voice, end in -ω *(o)* or -ώ *(o)*. This is
the ending with which they generally appear in dictionaries. Please
note that in everyday speech a more usual ending for -ώ *(o)* is
-άω *(ao)*. If a verb does not have an active voice form, in a dictionary it will appear with the ending -μαι *(-me)*, e.g. λυπάμαι
(leepame) **to be sad** or **sorry**, θυμάμαι *(theemame)* **to remember**.

The verb αγαπώ *aghapo* **to love** has typical endings for verbs ending in -ώ (*-o*) while those ending in -ω (*-o*) follow the pattern of έχω (*ekho*).

αγαπώ/άω (*aghapo/ao*)	**I love**
αγαπάς (*aghapas*)	**you love**
αγαπά (*aghapa*)	**he/she/it loves**
αγαπούμε (*aghapoome*)	**we love**
αγαπάτε (*aghapate*)	**you love**
αγαπούν (*aghapoon*)	**they love**

In Greek, there are two ways of addressing people, depending on their age, social or professional position, and how formal or informal the relationship is between two people. e.g. an older person will probably speak to a much younger one using the singular (informal way) but the younger person will use the plural (formal) unless well acquainted. Similarly two friends will speak to each other using the informal singular:

Τι κάνεις; (*tee kanees*)	**How are you?**
Καλά, εσύ; (*kala esee*)	**Fine, and you?**

While two acquaintances will address each other in a more formal way using the second person plural, like this:

Τι κάνετε; (*tee kanete*)	**How are you?**
Καλά, εσείς; (*kala esees*)	**Fine, and you?**

PERSONAL PRONOUNS

There are times when the pronoun needs to be used as e.g. in conjunction with the verb in order to establish the sex of the person involved, i.e. **he** or **she**, or indeed **it**.

εγώ	**I**	*egho*
εσύ	**you**	*esee*
αυτός	**he**	*aftos*
αυτή	**she**	*aftee*
αυτό	**it**	*afto*
εμείς	**we**	*emees*
εσείς	**you**	*esees*
αυτοί	**they** (*masc.*)	*aftee*
αυτές	**they** (*fem.*)	*aftes*
αυτά	**they** (*neut.*)	*afta*

Thus:	αυτός έχει (*aftos ekhee*)	**he has**
	αυτή έχει (*aftee ekhee*)	**she has**